I'M TIRED OF RACISM

True Stories of Existing While Black

By Sharon Hurley Hall

ISBN: 978-976-95469-1-2

Published by Lime Tree Media

Printed in the United States of America

Find out more about the author and her upcoming books online at https://www.sharonhh.com.

Cover design by Dan Walker of Dan Walker Creative LLC.

DEDICATION

This book is dedicated to my family, who support me — always. My mother, Kathleen; my sister, Lisa; my husband, Stephen; and my daughter, Taryn, are my biggest cheerleaders. Love you all, and thank you.

This book is also dedicated to the memory of George Floyd, Breonna Taylor, and all the Black lives lost to white supremacy. May you all rest in power.

CONTENTS

ACKNOWLEDGMENTS

Thanks to all the constant supporters of my anti-racism work, especially Alice Blackburn, Cathy Miller, Mitchell Allen, Kerstin Mortensen, Ruth Diaz, and Stephanie Schwab, who jumped in early to offer extra financial support for my anti-racism newsletter. Your faith in my efforts helped convince me I was on the right track.

Finally, this book wouldn't be the same without the editorial support of Cynthia Williams at Dragonfly Editorial.

FOREWORD
BY ASHANTI MAYA MARTIN

You know when you've been awake for so long, you get overtired? It happens when you are singularly focused on one thing because the stakes are high.

It's the feeling that sets in after staying up all night to write a term paper or cram for a final exam.

It is the feeling that people responding to natural and manmade disasters experience.

It's the feeling of staying up all night in the hospital, waiting for news of a loved one as they endure a health crisis or undergo a serious procedure.

After such endeavors, of course our body and mind need rest. However, cruelly, it is often at this point that rest evades us. Internally, our body chemistry makes rest challenging. Externally, life's rhythms and responsibilities go on regardless of our own circadian rhythms being disrupted. We want nothing more than to rest and to go to sleep, but the adrenaline and hormones won't let us.

We're so tired we can't sleep.

In 2022, so many of us Black people are overtired, but we can't go back to sleep. Life since 2020 has been a relentless push toward ushering in understanding and combating injustice. I met Sharon, virtually, that summer. She first appeared in my orbit on LinkedIn, where a cluster of

Black people began transforming the platform into a space to speak hard truths to the "executive class," who couldn't easily escape uncomfortable conversations in the Covid-era digital watercooler.

Sharon and I are both career writers who for decades had applied our craft and creativity toward amplifying and enriching the power structures in which we operated by default, for survival and in pursuit of a life of relative and small comforts. We both found reward and enjoyment in these careers, but in 2020 it suddenly wasn't good enough. Our paths intersected right around the moment that the two of us and so many others began to wake up became determined to align our creative and intellectual capital with the pursuit of facing racism head on, finally, pointedly, specifically, and loudly. No hedging. No more being quiet.

Sharon's Anti-Racism Newsletter seized on the drumbeat of events throughout the summer and leading up to the 2020 election. She also had a deep well of experience and perspective to draw from, and on a weekly schedule weaved analyses of systemic racism and her personal encounters with racism to illustrate how these factors play off each other on a daily basis.

Sharon's Anti-Racism Newsletter is a terrific read in your inbox. As a compilation, I'm Tired Of Racism is a volume that allows you to take in all of Sharon's reflections and contemplate the individual experiences of a Black woman in 2022.

By dedicating her craft to anti-racism, Sharon is living her own advice and showing how each of us can do more, now. The days of waiting for a leader to speak on behalf of the Black community in the U.S. and the

Black diaspora are over. We don't need to wait for someone with a megaphone who can take a stage and rouse people across this nation and the world. It is on ***us*** to stand up and speak out against injustice and about our lived experience.

Because Sharon's experience is rooted in the U.S., the Caribbean, and Europe, she's able to tell us how the U.S. looks from the outside in (not great at the moment), and explain how even being a citizen of a Black-majority country comes with its own layered burdens rooted in colonialism and white supremacy.

As Sharon writes unequivocally, "the era of the quiet Black woman is over." Implicit in this statement and something that still seems to vex people is that we were keeping our mouths shut for far too long. News flash: Racism existed before 2020, was a problem before George Floyd died, and is something that your coworkers, colleagues, and community members experienced literally every day.

It should not be that hard to imagine that racism does not only exist under the knee of a cop empowered by his license to kill a man and get away with it because the victim is Black. Racism doesn't only hang from trees. It doesn't only wear a white hood, it doesn't only wear blackface, and it doesn't only shout epithets.

Yes, in the 21st century, racism still happens to Black people every day; we've just been quiet about it. Things have improved so much since the civil rights era. Why should we complain? Now all we have to do is work hard and rely on the legions of "colorblind" people to judge us by our character and not our skin, hair, or accents.

And yet, we've seen the long list of things one can't do while being Black. Playing, driving, eating, sleeping, working, existing. The palpable fear of people passing you by on the street, the looks of shock when a hiring panel sees that your face doesn't match what they thought was a "white" name, or talented students on elite college campuses being treated as the help. For so many, every day is filled with small indignities that can lead to damage of physical, emotional, mental, and spiritual wellness.

It. Is. Tiring.

If Sharon's writings are the first time you are peeking into the life of a Black woman in the 21st century, please read, listen, and learn. Understand that not only these experiences, but the act of recounting them and rehashing them, require work, strenuous work. Be a part of the solution, share some of the burden, and dedicate yourself to unlearning racism. Take up your own mantle so that others may get some rest.

Ashanti Maya Martin is a professional writer, creative strategist, and visionary activist. She is the author of the famous New York Times article "Black LinkedIn Is Thriving. Does LinkedIn Have a Problem With That?"

INTRODUCTION: WHY I'M NO LONGER A QUIET BLACK WOMAN

Ever notice that when you change something about yourself, there are people who don't like it? I've seen that happen a few times, and I'm confidently expecting it to happen now. That's because I'm no longer a quiet Black woman.

In the past, quiet has been my thing. I'm an introvert, and observing from the shadows is my comfort zone. I have a lot of thoughts, but only a few people ever get to hear them. That applies to a lot of topics, including racism.

Like most Black people, I've been aware of and have experienced racism throughout my life. Sometimes it looks different, depending on where I am, but I always know how to recognize it. Whether I'm at work or at leisure, it's always there. And even when I'm sitting at home, in a country where most people look like me, there's still the issue of how Black people are represented in the media. Until recently, conversations about these topics were reserved for the inner, inner circle.

But then things changed. The police murdered George Floyd, and I found I couldn't keep quiet any longer.

That cold-blooded murder unlocked something in me, and I finally started sharing those thoughts with the world, on all the platforms where I have a presence.

I didn't know what would happen. If I thought about it at all, I figured

I might lose a few contacts and miss out on a couple of jobs. Maybe I have, but if they've disappeared, I haven't noticed.

What's surprised me is the number of people who are ready to listen and ready to act. I've seen white friends commit to being anti-racist, to having hard conversations with their peers, to amplifying Black voices, and to sharing resources that support the anti-racism battle.

White friends have checked in with me to make sure they hadn't said anything stupid in the past. As I pointed out, if I cared about them at all, we probably had the conversation at the time. And if we're still friends, it's because we resolved whatever it was.

One friend struggles with some of the messages I amplify — for example, a social media post urging would-be white anti-racist activists not to ask their Black friends things they can learn from Google. I'm at a loss as to why this one friend is so troubled by this. If you took the racism component out of it and said, "Don't ask your techie friend something you could learn from Google," it would be inoffensive. So why does it become a problem when we're talking about racism?

What has thrilled me about all of this is seeing so many others find their voices and speak their truth.

As for myself, I don't think I can stop now. There's too much work to do, and it will take time. I have been lucky enough to get the gift of writing, and telling Black stories is how I will support anti-racist action. The age of the quiet Black woman is over.

1
WHILE BLACK: THOUGHTS ON THE ASSUMPTION OF WRONGNESS

When I think about the Black Death, these days I don't think about the medieval plague. Instead, I relate the label to the widespread killing of Black people in America. Some people might not understand why a non-American even cares about this. But Black people in a post-slavery or post-colonial context have all suffered the enduring effects of racial discrimination, so we feel every incident as if it happens to us.

Here in the Caribbean, many of us have Black relatives who are or have become American, or who attend school there. I certainly do. Simply put, I'm scared for those relatives, and many Caribbean people feel the same.

The danger of existing while Black in the US has been proved time and time again. A short list of the most recent victims (including George Floyd, Breonna Taylor, Ahmaud Arbery, Elijah McClain, Sandra Bland, Trayvon Martin) reminds us of the potential harm, but there have been many, many more over decades.

In so many cases, to be Black is to be in the wrong, before you do anything or open your mouth. #AhmaudArbery

If I were in the US, my word about my own probity wouldn't be enough to save me from being stopped by the police, arrested, or killed.

Sure, racism exists everywhere. I've had some experiences in the UK that would make your toes curl. I've experienced discrimination in the

Caribbean. But I never felt like any of those incidents would result in my death. That's not the case for Black people in the US. That's why parents have to have "the talk" with their children about what to do if you're stopped by the police, about why your hands must be in sight, about how you need to ask permission for every move, lest it be misconstrued. I had to have the talk with my daughter when she went to college in the US. The trigger-happy minority has ruined things for everyone.

The deadly potential of American racism is why Black mothers and dads have their hearts in their mouths as their sons grow up and go out in the world. They know there's no guarantee the boys will be safe in the US. As we've seen, even being in your own home, minding your business, won't keep you alive. But parents of daughters are afraid, too — your gender doesn't protect you. #SandraBland

A good friend of mine said, "I am not sending my beautiful Black child to the US to be shot!" That child will be going to school in Canada or the UK, where his skin color isn't a death sentence.

Will it ever change? Who knows? Because the thing is, the concept — and it is only a concept — of whiteness depends on making Blackness an "other." Back in the days of slavery and colonialism, in order for racist white people to sleep at night, they created and perpetuated a fiction that Black people still live with — and die from — today. As *Orientalism* author Edward Said says, "Every empire, however, tells itself and the world that it is unlike all other empires, that its mission is not to plunder and control but to educate and liberate."

That's how people justify colonialism and neo-colonialism (it's not about the oil or other resources at all, clearly).

Underlying all of this is the uncomfortable fact that the white establishment needed Black people, yet still didn't want to value us. When slavery ended by force in the US, ex-slaveholding states turned right around and criminalized minor infractions to create an imprisoned workforce, slavery by another name. Watch Netflix's *13TH* — it's pretty instructive.

But even the people who were "on our side" saw us as less than, in a different way. Some liberals are only liberal when Black people need help, but still don't see us as equals. I've had personal experience of this with a former colleague.

I'm tired of this. Black people are tired of this. Tired of doing everything "the right way" only to learn that it's still wrong. Tired of being castigated when we take a different route to make our voices heard. (I guess those who don't like it when we kneel aren't going to like it when we stand and demand justice.) And, most of all, tired of dying needlessly. Didn't enough of us do that during enslavement, while white slave owners built personal, generational, and national wealth? Enough already!

So what's next? It's clear that Black people can't fix racism alone. It's been proved time and again that whatever we say about it hardly counts. So it's up to white people to play their part. First of all, acknowledge the system, described eloquently by Scott Woods:

> *Yes, racism looks like hate, but hate is just one manifestation. Privilege is another. Access is another. Ignorance is another. Apathy is another. And so on. So while I agree with people who say no one is born racist, it remains a powerful system that we're immediately born into. It's like being born into air: you take it in as soon as you breathe. It's not a cold that you can get over. There is no anti-racist certification class. It's a set of socioeconomic traps and cultural values that are fired up every time we interact with the world. It is a thing you have to keep scooping out of the boat of your life to keep from drowning in it. I know it's hard work, but it's the price you pay for owning everything.*

Second, don't sit in silence bemoaning the system. Do something. Here's what my *Introvert Sisters* podcast co-host Lisa Hurley says:

> *As my math teachers would say: "Show your work" It is not enough to think or say that you're not a racist. Demonstrate active anti-racism. Silence and inaction = complicity. Get uncomfortable. Stay uncomfortable. Make an effort. Educate yourself. Take action. Show solidarity in public. Get out of our DMs and onto your feeds. Your silence is deafening. Your need to be co-signed as "one of the good ones" is burdensome. We are not here to hold space for you at this time. If you are feeling triggered and defensive reading this, then you are who it is meant for. #dothework*

If you do the work, maybe one day existing while Black will be the norm and not a crime.

CALLS TO ARMS

Some days the anti-racism drum beats loudly in my head. That's when I write pieces like the next few, articles that show the awfulness of racism, driving the point home repeatedly.

2
I'M TIRED (OF RACISM)

There are so many reasons why it's time for racism to end

I'm a Black woman, but sometimes I don't speak about race and racism. Because I'm tired …

I'm tired of the color of my skin being a reason to stop me from my daily rounds or being, in the US, a mark of death.

I'm tired of the name-calling. The first time someone called me a n****r, I was six or seven. I can still remember the sting. I've been called that word in multiple languages, and it hurts in all of them.

I'm tired of the "problem" of my hair. The nun who ran my primary school in the '70s took exception to my afro. "Is it clean; is it neat?" asked my dad. "If the answer is yes, we have nothing to talk about." I remember interviewing for a job in the '80s and being told I'd have to do something about my braided hair if I got the job. Everyone else in the world can wear their hair the way it grows from their head. What makes our hair so different?

I'm tired of the double take when I walk into an interview. My name could be that of a blue-eyed lass from Ireland. They weren't expecting to see me. One colleague complained that my name "wasn't African enough." Who asked her, anyway?

I'm tired of the reduced expectations — the people who think I'm of lesser intelligence (trust me, I'm not!) and the ones who assume I'll only be interested in Black issues. I'm a human being, and this is my planet. So stuff it! Plus, I'm a polymath — I'm interested in a bunch of things.

I'm tired of people taking one look at my profile picture and thinking I'm worth less, or even worthless. Despite my having two MAs and more than 30 years of writing experience, some people want to pay me less than they pay entry-level colleagues from outside the Diaspora. I'm not taking it, though. I value myself, even if some don't value me.

I'm tired of the coverage — the crackheads, thugs, mammies, pimps, and drug dealers, all of whom were supposed to represent people like me, until a couple of decades ago. And even though coverage is better, there are still plenty of those portrayals shaping how people see us. (Why did Denzel win his Oscar for portraying a dirty cop rather than for any of the other fine characters he played? He was an awesome Malcolm X, but I guess that was too much of a threat?)

I'm tired of the "it was a long time ago." Systemic oppression has no expiry date.

I'm tired of the "I'm not racist because …" If you're not explicitly anti-racist, you're part of the problem.

I'm tired of feeling like if I say how I really feel about inequity and lack of diversity, people will stereotype me as an "angry Black woman." Yes, I'm a Black woman, and I'm angry about these issues, but it's not the same thing.

I'm tired of more than 50 years of this shit for me, and 400 years of it for people who look like me.

I'm tired of having to educate people who can read and learn about everything else in the world but white privilege, racism, and history. Please, just #dothework

When it comes to racism (overt aggressions and microaggressions), there are a lot more things I'm tired of, but mostly I'm just tired.

3
LET'S DISCARD THE NOTION

Unlearn these ideas to commit to anti-racism without stressing out your Black friends

Let's discard the notion that when Black people tell white people to Google stuff about racism before asking a Black person, they are being unhelpful or shutting down conversation.

NO! We are simply asking you to **do some work as a basis for a more informed conversation about race, racism, and anti-racism**. The same way you Google your symptoms before you see your doctor, see if resources already exist before putting your Black friends through more pain.

*

Let's discard the notion that just because you're only now learning of the horror of racism, you should be able to pick over and discuss it ad nauseam with your Black friends as you begin to unlearn long-held assumptions.

NO! We ingested that trauma with our mother's milk, have lived it for decades, and don't need to rehash the pain to convince you that it is wrong or show you how bad it is. **WE already know, so it's up to you, white people, to do that work.**

*

Let's discard the notion that your need for information trumps Black people's need for self-care.

NO! Sometimes it's too much and Black, Indigenous, and People of Color (**BIPOC) need to prioritize their mental and emotional health**. Check out your white friends who are already doing the work, or do some more Googling and reading.

*

Let's discard the notion that there's one right way — or one white way — to dismantle white supremacy.

NO! No revolution is quiet and peaceful. Like Rep. John Lewis said, **it's time to make good trouble**, and sometimes that means protesting, being vocal, being noisy, being in your face and, most of all, never giving up.

*

Let's discard the notion that your one Black friend or colleague speaks for all Black people.

NO! **BIPOC people are not a monolith**. While we have many shared experiences, we have many individual ones. So what's true for one may not be true for all.

*

Let's discard the notion that when we say, "Black lives matter," we mean only Black lives matter.

NO! We mean Black lives matter too. We mean all lives won't matter until Black lives matter. We mean stop the microaggressions, stop the discrimination, stop the bigotry, stop the inequity, and stop killing us, FFS.

*

Let's discard the notion that when we say, "Dismantle white supremacy," it means Black people and BIPOC hate all white people.

NO! **We hate racists and perpetrators of inequity**. If you are one of the "good white folks," as antiracism writer Marley K. says, you have nothing to worry about. If you are actively anti-racist, you have nothing to worry about, even if you make the occasional mistake.

*

Let's discard the notion that equity for BIPOC means we're taking something away from white people.

NO! **We're asking for what's fair and just** in countries that were built from the profits of our enforced labor.

*

Let's discard the notion that white privilege is the purview of rich and prominent white folks, and only them.

NO! White privilege is about not facing discrimination because of your skin color. Not being followed around stores. Not receiving sub-standard schooling, redlined housing. Not fearing death if you interact with the police. **If your skin is white, you have that privilege**.

*

Let's discard the notion that Black people's character is enough reason for their death at the hands of the police.

NO! **Afford Black people the same grace that white people get**.

Why does a Black person's history taint the whole race, while a white criminal is a lone wolf?

Why is a Black person's history evidence of bad character that justifies their death while a white person's history is evidence of mental illness?

Why do Black suspects die while white criminals like Dylann Roof get Burger King?

See the problem? We need equity in these areas and in everything.

*

Let's discard the notion that white fragility and tears are more important than Black people's pain.

NO! If you are a white person committed to anti-racism, **accept that it's going to get uncomfortable** and you won't like everything you hear.

*

Let's discard the notion that your white discomfort with Black people speaking their truth as they see fit is enough reason for them to stop and massage their message to make you feel better.

NO! We have been silent for too long, and **doing it your way has obviously not worked.** Now it's time for BIPOC to be more vocal, to share more, to amplify messages from non-traditional sources, so that nobody has an excuse for not knowing what's happening, how we feel, or what to do about it.

*

Let's discard the notion that dismantling racism is primarily a Black concern.

NO! **It's everybody's business** — and it's nobody's business more than the white people who started it all. As Catherine Pugh, Esq., says, "Racism is not mine, it's yours, and it's not called 'help' when it's your mess we're cleaning."

Hear me now: if you're a committed anti-racist, discard all of those notions. Then do the work.

4
I CAN'T IGNORE RACISM; CAN YOU?

There's no getting back to normal until racism ends

When George Floyd was murdered — and it will never be anything else *but* murder — there was outrage across races and even countries. Social media lit up with black squares and promises to do better. White "allies" appeared out of nowhere. Companies with troubled pasts hastened to say something, *anything*, about diversity, equity, and inclusion.

But after just one year — though there were still lots of people, Black and white, fighting the good fight (thank you; we see you) — many "allies" burned out. Many companies went back to business as usual. For many white people, fighting racism for more than a few weeks was too much or too hard. Imagine how we BIPOC feel.

As a Black person, I don't have that privilege. Your cause of the day is my *life* and many Black lives.

Here are some other privileges I don't have when I move in spaces where I am "minoritized":

I don't have the privilege of being seen as simply "Sharon." I move through the world with the almost unbearable weight of white gazes, ancient stereotypes, and low expectations.

I don't have the privilege of walking tall, unfettered by the color of my skin, in a world where many white people want to make me less than I am. (By the way, I refuse.)

I don't have the privilege of ignoring the impact of the color of my skin on white people in the street, in workplaces, and in everyday life.

I don't have the privilege of overlooking the fact that being in the wrong place at the wrong time could kill my Black brothers and sisters, my Black child, or me.

I don't have the privilege of forgetting that so many countries were built on — and grew rich on — our enslaved labor, yet we still aren't truly free and have never received compensation. (Though, I ask you, what could really compensate for being trafficked, enslaved, discriminated against, despised, deprived, and hated?)

I don't have the privilege of always seeing people who look like me *and* represent my reality on TV and in the media. (Yes, I'm still mad that Denzel won his Oscar for *Training Day*, and Halle for *Monster's Ball.* I'm not knocking the quality of their acting, but that quality was evident in many roles that didn't involve crime or alcoholism.)

I don't have the privilege of staying quiet when racists are actively discriminating against people who look like me. If I don't speak up, who will?

I don't have the privilege of ignoring racists' attempts to invalidate my looks, my education, my presence, and my very self.

I don't have the privilege of questioning whether this or that person meant to be racist. I know the impact, I feel the impact, and I always recognize racism.

I don't have the privilege of withdrawing from the fight to dismantle white supremacy. Black lives depend on all of us doing our part.

I don't have the privilege of waiting around till the death of another Black man causes another wave of outrage. One more Black death at the hands of the police is one Black death too many.

*

So, no, **I don't have the privilege**, the luxury, the option of going back to normal.

Nor do I want that privilege.

I want white people to begin to understand what it feels like to be in Black skin (you will never understand fully, but empathy is a start).

I want white people to look racism in the eye. I want them to do something about it and to be actively anti-racist.

And if they don't, I want them to realize and acknowledge that they are choosing to ignore racism and turn away from doing the work.

The white world doesn't give me the privilege of ignoring the color of my skin.

And so the white world should not have the privilege of ignoring racism, a problem that white people started and that white people should finish.

5
NOT ALL BLACK PEOPLE ...

One of the favorite tactics of racists and those who aren't real allies is to say "not all white people." Believe me, Black people already know, because if it were all white people, even more of us would probably be dead. But there's a lot white people don't know about Black people — a lot of assumptions they need to unlearn. And so I present: not all Black people ...

Not all Black people speak for each other. We have varied backgrounds and experiences, and we are not a monolith. That means there are Black people reading this right now who will disagree with me, and that's OK.

Not all Black people were enslaved in America starting in 1619; Black people were enslaved throughout the 17th century across the Americas.

Not all Black people participated in enslaving their peers. And if Europeans hadn't created a market, enslavement would never have become an inherited condition.

Not all Black people know their history, especially if educated in white-majority countries.

Not all Black people love the skin they're in. Enslavement, colonialism, and a whole heap of trouble lets you understand why some passed for white if they could and why colorism still divides some Black communities.

Not all Black people hate the skin they're in. Few do. They just wish more people would let them be in that skin in peace.

Not all Black people love their hair; many have been socialized to see it as a "problem" that has to be "managed." Mistreatment at work and school just reinforces this perception.

Not all Black people hate their hair. Some see it as a beloved crown, letting them walk tall and acknowledge their ancestry. For them, Black hair is part of Black beauty and something to be cherished.

Not all Black people are OK with Black people using the N-word, let alone white people — even if they're singing it. (Similarly, not all Black people hate it with a passion; some even want to "reclaim" it.)

Not all Black people have names that "sound Black," whatever that means. Thanks to enslavement and colonization, not to mention rape and cultural erasure, many of us have names that sound like the names of the people who enslaved and brutalized us. And ain't that a mind trip, if you stop to think about it.

Not all Black people are educational underachievers. Despite discriminatory systems, many people rise, achieve, and excel.

Not all Black people speak African American Vernacular English (AAVE), not even all Black Americans. It depends on your upbringing.

Not all Black people speak in dialect or patois. First of all, these so-called "dialects" are Creole languages. Second, because of colonialism, many Black people, in the former British Caribbean at least, speak standard English most of the time.

Not all Black people are poor. Some are, a few are super-rich, and the rest are muddling along in the middle.

Not all Black people can be Oprah or Barack Obama. Very few can, and when those few succeed, look at the backlash. Was it so bad that you had to elect an orange man-child?

Not all Black people are strong. We can't bear more, physically or emotionally, than people of other races. We feel pain, we cry, and we suffer just like everyone else. Just like white people, we may need medication or counseling, though we're less likely to get it.

Not all Black people are cisgender. Black people have a range of gender identities and expressions, and all Black lives matter.

Not all Black people are able-bodied or neurotypical. Some have physical and mental disabilities, and not all of these are visible. So, please, give people some grace.

Not all Black people live in daily fear of being shot by the police; that dubious honor is mostly reserved for Black people in America.

Not all Black people live in the inner city. Many live in the burbs, though they'd still better be careful if they're walking or jogging.

Not all Black people use or sell drugs, but those who do get stiffer sentences than their white peers doing the same thing.

Not all Black people carry guns; so why is this always a suspicion?

Besides, no Black person would walk up to the cops carrying an AK-47 and expect to live. #justsayin

Not all Black people have bootstraps to pull themselves up by; centuries of enslavement don't create much scope for amassing generational wealth.

Not all Black people are athletic; some of us are klutzes too. (Yours truly is a case in point; I can trip over nothing.)

Not all Black people are bad; many do lots of good quietly.

Not all Black people fight injustice by marching; some of us use the power of the pen (keyboard?) to educate and inspire.

Not all Black people will fight this anti-racism battle quietly; some will be loud and in your face.

Not all Black people fight racism all the time. Though they're often affected by racism all the time, they also have to earn a living.

Not all Black people want to educate white people about racism; many are too tired of living it to want to talk about it.

Not all Black people will give time to white fragility; put on your adult panties and learn (and you can cut out the tears, too).

Not all Black people trust white people's word. Actions speak louder, and consistent action shouts. Doing the work is right and just, so don't be looking for cookies, either.

The next time you find yourself buying into a bias or stereotype, just check yourself. And remember: **not all Black people** …

6
DO BLACK LIVES REALLY MATTER?

I say they do, but the system keeps trying to prove me wrong

Since the police officers who murdered her have not been charged, there is no justice for Breonna Taylor. Just like there is no justice for so, so many dead Black people.

The list of Black people who need justice and fail to get it is long and growing longer each decade, each year, each month, each week, and, sometimes, each day.

Over the decades, there have been thousands of Black people killed or maimed by the forces that are supposed to protect all of us.

But Black people don't usually get that protection. I don't feel the same safety as white people do when they see the police.

It's hard.

As a Black woman, I'm hurting because no matter how often I tell myself that Black lives matter, the system makes it crystal clear that they don't, that *my* life doesn't matter.

Every time an unarmed Black man or woman ends up dead, it tells me I don't matter.

Every time the fact of Blackness or a Black person's history is used to justify that death, it tells me I don't matter.

Every time the system fails to indict killers for murdering Black people, it tells me I don't matter.

Every time video evidence of the killing of Black people isn't enough to secure justice, it tells me I don't matter.

Every time another Black teen gets stigmatized for being a kid, it tells me I don't matter.

Every time Black people are castigated for the same behavior white people get away with, it tells me I don't matter.

Every time Black people and white people with identical circumstances are treated differently by the media, by law enforcement, by the "justice" system, by the educational system, by the companies we work for, it tells me I don't matter.

Every time Black people can't walk, talk, jog, attend school, drive a nice car, go to work, or live ordinary daily life without being in danger, it tells me I don't matter.

Every time people see the destruction of property as more important than the destruction of Black lives, it tells me I don't matter.

Every time a white person targets me with microaggressions and outright racism, it tells me I don't matter.

Every time my white colleagues stand by while others discriminate, it tells me I don't matter.

Every time our white friends, acquaintances, and colleagues fail to call out obviously racist actions, it tells me I don't matter.

Every time someone gaslights my lived experience of racism, it tells me I don't matter.

Every time Black history is whitewashed, diminished, or denied, it tells me I don't matter.

Every time diversity efforts are ignored or undermined, it tells me I don't matter.

Every time the trolls and racists come for me, it tells me I don't matter.

Every time my voice is suppressed on social media, it tells me I don't matter.

My Black life doesn't matter to the system, and it doesn't matter to many individuals.

Yes, there are allies, advocates, and supporters. Their voices are getting louder. Their actions are getting noticed.

But the system is bigger than all of us, and it tells me — and us — Black lives don't matter.

I *know* Black lives matter, and sometimes I am still discouraged by the long, sticky tentacles of systemic racism.

But I don't let that stop me.

I may get despondent today, but tomorrow — and all the tomorrows — I will get up again and keep writing, talking, sharing, and fighting because what matters is changing minds about the value of Black lives. What matters is ending racism.

I urge you to stand with me, and let all of us actively declare by our words and our actions:

Black lives do matter.

Black lives do matter.

Black lives do matter.

Maybe one day everyone will know it's true.

7
SOMETIMES, I CAN'T ...

Aspects of racism may be unbelievable, but they're very real

Here's a little something that popped into my head on a morning walk. You know how we say, "I just can't"? Well, here are some things I can't believe:

Sometimes, I can't believe I have to read about another Black person dying, and I definitely can't watch the videos. So please don't send them.

Sometimes I can't believe I have to suffer another racist incident, but I do it anyway. Sometimes I'm weary of it all, and I'm not alone.

Sometimes, I can't believe the US elected a racist bully who's terrorizing the world — and how many people were prepared to let him do it again. Supposedly white supremacists are a dying breed, but it sounds to me like somebody's lying.

Sometimes I can't believe that advocating for equity and against white supremacy can get me banned on social media, but if a white person pushes back against Black Lives Matter and racial justice, it's fair comment. Something's wrong there, for sure.

Sometimes, I can't believe how many racists there are on social media and that, even on professional networks, they're not afraid to speak out.

Sometimes I can't believe that companies think that hiring a white woman ticks the diversity box.

Sometimes I can't believe the hidden "one in, one out" policy that leaves Black people alone and unsupported in some workplaces.

Sometimes I can't believe how excessively qualified Black people have to be to get the same opportunity as an unqualified white colleague.

Sometimes I can't believe I still have to explain basic facts about history to educated people who know how to use Google.

Sometimes I can't believe how many white people blame Black people for racism, a problem we didn't start and can't end.

Sometimes I can't believe how many Black people don't identify with Black people's problems, but then I remember internalized racism and I do.

Sometimes I can't believe my privilege as an educated Black woman is not enough to keep me alive in the wrong circumstances.

Sometimes I can't believe white people don't, won't, or can't see racism.

Sometimes I can't believe that people can't put themselves in others' shoes and see how they would feel.

Sometimes I can't believe the mealymouthed language that couches racism and oppression, though I guess white supremacists have had centuries of practice.

Sometimes I can't believe that nearly 200 years after the end of enslavement in the Caribbean, we are still dealing with the fallout, and that those with the most privilege want us to get over it.

Sometimes I can't believe that there are still those who see equity as taking something from them.

Sometimes I can't believe that I still have to argue that racism and equity are human rights issues and not political ones.

Sometimes I can't believe that even though the world is better for some Black people, it's not better enough.

Sometimes I can't believe I have to write about this again, but I must, or how will it end?

I must believe one day racism will end, but sometimes I can't.

BARBADIANA

I'm very much a Caribbean woman, and I count Barbados as one of my homes. It's where I received most of my education, but having lived abroad for many years, I am also able to approach it as an outsider and take a more objective view of the issues of racism and colorism we face here. Of course, as a dark-skinned Black woman, I'm not totally impartial, but these next essays share some insights.

8
BLACK LIVES MATTER AND THE BARBADIAN CONTEXT

Why we need to have difficult conversations about our history

Some time ago, I attended a Black Lives Matter march in Barbados. If you know anything about Barbados, and much of the Caribbean, you probably know that Black people are in the majority. So why would Barbadians even need such a march? There are lots of answers to this question, but in the end, it comes down to three things:

A shared history of enslavement: Since Barbados was one of the earliest slave societies in the 17th century, the southern states in the US used the Barbados slave code as a model for their own reign of terror.

Family ties: Many Caribbean families have Black relatives and friends in the US. I have three relatives there, two of them male, so I'm very aware of the dangers they face.

A recognition that **we have not really dealt with the legacy of enslavement and colonialism in the Caribbean:** As I discuss in my book *Exploring Shadeism,* many of our ideas about ethnicity result from that poisoned seed.

Because of this, the murder of George Floyd and the deaths of other Black people at the hands of the US police have sparked many discussions. That's because many of the biases against Black or dark-skinned people that exist in white-majority countries also permeate our culture.

In Barbados, despite the optics (a Black prime minister, Black government ministers, some Black business owners, and a huge array of Black professionals), the descendants of plantation owners still wield the most financial muscle. The compensation they got for the loss of the people they enslaved has translated into multi-generational wealth.

As a result, they can easily afford the best for their family members, whereas less-well-off people may have to struggle. Some of these descendants still have a superiority complex, while others resent them for it.

Black Barbadians and white Barbadians rarely mix beyond what's necessary to get things done. While there are exceptions, there's a kind of de facto apartheid that takes place, starting with school.

Black people and white people mix in the classroom, but when they socialize during break time and lunchtime, it's usually with people who look like them. It happened in my parents' time, in my time, and now in my daughter's time, though her own friend group is diverse.

Outside the classroom, Black and white Barbadians usually socialize separately. They may come together over a sporting event, but you won't often see them in each other's homes.

As recently as the 1980s, there were places that didn't welcome dark-skinned Barbadians, and as recently as the early 2000s, I witnessed the manager of a beach club berate Barbadians (who were availing themselves of the free, public beach) for mooching off the club's facilities. The whites who actually were mooching heard nothing from him.

(The irony is that post–COVID-19, with tourism at an all-time low, the club is trying to attract local traffic. But locals have long memories, and the club has removed its Facebook page after scads of negative comments on the issue.)

So the George Floyd murder raised loads of issues, and one of those involves a statue. Specifically, a statue of Lord Horatio Nelson (a product of his time — and therefore a racist), which until 2020 stood at the head of the island's main shopping street, in what used to be called Trafalgar Square. (Apparently, it predates the one in London by a few years.)

The area is now called National Heroes Square, and as many have pointed out, Nelson is not a hero to us. Calls to "Take down Nelson" have become increasingly more strident. Just as loud are the voices calling for the statue to remain because of its historical value (plus, taking down a statue could be seen as a performative action and a replacement for actually addressing the remaining inequities in our country).

In the past, I admit, I haven't felt strongly about this. But now I think that the proper place for that statue is in the Barbados Museum, in an exhibit that details the good *and* the bad of Nelson.[1]

More importantly, it is beyond sad that it took video evidence of white bias to focus white attention around the world on what Black people have known for centuries.

---

[1] The statue was finally removed in November 2020 and will be placed in the museum.

So let's not lessen the impact of the murders of George Floyd, Breonna Taylor, and dozens of other cut-short lives in a series of performative actions.

Instead, let's put their murderers on trial and take action to actually improve Black people's lives. In the US, that means training the police better. It means funding community services that can deal with non-criminal matters. And it means ending the practice of weaponizing whiteness by pretending to see a threat where none exists. ("Karens," I'm looking at you.)

And here in Barbados, it means having those difficult conversations about privilege, responsibility, and equity. It's the only way we can all move forward.

9
TOWARD A MORE EQUITABLE BARBADOS: WHY BLACK LIVES MATTER TO US

Black people matter to Black people — here's why

Whenever the question of Black Lives Matter comes up in Barbados, there's the inevitable question: why do we need such a movement in a place where Black people are in the majority? As with most things, it's not quite that simple.

Let's get one thing out of the way: as someone said recently, "Black bodies matter to people with Black bodies." In part, this is because of our shared history. In the Caribbean and America, Black people were enslaved, trafficked, and forced to labor, unpaid. We had our history of being kings, queens, and members of ancient and great civilizations obliterated, and our cultures derided. Centuries later, this left a trauma from which we have never recovered, and we're still dealing with the societal fallout.

We also have current family ties. Many Caribbean people have Black relatives and friends in the US, the UK, and other places where the color of our skin affects how we are viewed and treated. So when shots are fired against Black people in the US, the echoes resonate around the world, wherever Black people live. When there's a knee on someone's neck, we, too, can't breathe. This happens too often, and we fear it will keep happening.

Here's another factor: in most post-colonial societies, we have never dealt with the legacy of enslavement and the years that followed our supposed freedom. How easy is it to be free after centuries of being regarded as less than human? How easy is it to be free after centuries of being denied education? How easy is it to be free without the resources our enslavers took for granted? When white people were "pulling themselves up by their bootstraps," they were also ensuring that Black enslaved and recently freed people had no boots.

The proof that there's still a lot to deal with is everywhere you look. It's in the language of colorism, which privileges lighter skin shades and "good hair." It's in the separate lives Black and white Barbadians live, outside of school, work, or sports. It's in the places where Black people historically weren't welcome and the places where they still aren't welcome. So, yes, Black lives matter in the Caribbean as much as anywhere, because we still have a long way to go.

One further proof of the long journey is the panic caused among some white Barbadians when it was suggested that we support Black-owned businesses for a single day.

You have to wonder why this action is so threatening. After all, a single day of support won't change the fact that most of the financial muscle remains in the hands of descendants of the plantocracy. It doesn't change the fact that most businesses are owned by descendants of the plantocracy.

Maybe it's guilt, because, after all, the financial stability of white Barbadians was created via the enslaved labor of Black Barbadians. And it was secured by the payments made to former enslavers by colonial governments. That can't sit well with any anti-racist white person.

Perhaps this suggestion caused such a stir because taking action debunks the idea that Bajans are "good" Black people who don't rock the boat. As more learned people than I have established, there were uprisings, rebellions, and riots throughout the period of enslavement and beyond. No one submits willingly to being made less than.

Maybe white people were upset because they know the power of supporting your own, as they have done for centuries. If Black people did the same, where does that leave their businesses? There's power in numbers, and it means white business owners can no longer take for granted the support of Black shoppers. In the current environment, businesses that actively discriminate against their employees or customers, or those that have racist owners or employees, are being called out publicly.

But I think there was such an uproar because there's no way to justify the unjustifiable: enslavement was wrong, failure to repair the damage to Black people was wrong, and racism is wrong. Those who believe otherwise are on the wrong side of history.

But history also shows that unless we start to take action, nothing will change. Supporting Black businesses for a day or a weekend only serves to highlight the inequities we still need to address and the work we need to do to urge all Barbadians to do better to create a more equitable society.

10
SIX REASONS TO RAISE YOUR BIPOC KIDS IN BLACK-MAJORITY COUNTRIES

Why this mother of one felt the pros outweighed the cons

I have a British-born biracial daughter. And when my English husband and I had to decide where to raise her, we decided to go to Barbados, in the Caribbean. I'm lucky enough to hold dual citizenship, which made the decision easier.

Having talked to Black friends who went to school in England, there was a common theme: it wasn't easy. In fact, sometimes they had awful experiences of racism, from being called the N-word and followed around by kids making monkey noises to being excluded from all social gatherings by fellow students. I heard similar stories from my Black American friends.

As her parents, we had to weigh up the value of great educational and career opportunities in the UK (which I benefited from as an adult) against endemic institutional racism (in education, in policing, and elsewhere).

And we also had to balance the post-enslavement legacy in Barbados against the value of being in the majority.

In the end, it wasn't a hard decision. Like many of my British-born friends, we felt there was more to gain than to lose if my daughter grew up in the Caribbean. Here are six of the main advantages I see.

1. People Who Look Like Us

Black people are people of the global majority, but in many places in the UK and the US, I can go weeks and months without seeing another Black face. In some schools and workplaces, mine is the lone Black countenance, and I immediately stand out as different and strange.

When I lived in the UK, one thing I loved about returning to the Caribbean was the anonymity. It's how white people move through the world in places where they're in the majority. When I'm in a country where Black people are in the majority, the color of my skin lets me blend in rather than stand out. It's a welcome relief after moving in spaces where I'm minoritized.

2. There Are Good Role Models

Not only are there people who look like me, but they do all sorts of jobs. There are more educators, doctors, lawyers, accountants, politicians, and prominent citizens than you can count. There are even Black business owners, though there's still some work to do there.

Under the surface, the descendants of plantation owners still carry a lot of financial weight. However, the optics are telling. Growing up in Barbados, I didn't think that prominent roles were barred to me or that I'd have to face huge obstacles to achieve them.

3. A Non-discriminatory Education System

Consciousness about race starts in school. In the UK, BIPOC

children are more likely to be excluded from education than white kids. In the US, you have the school-to-prison pipeline. In many parts of the Caribbean, we have the realization that education is our ticket to a better life.

Sure, I've still had to deal with colorism and classism and "hairism" (you can't take all the "isms" out of humans, unfortunately). But I didn't get shut out of education because of the color of my skin. Unlike the US and UK, Black excellence isn't newsworthy. In many schools, it's expected.

4. A More Balanced View of History

Delving into education a bit more, I've noticed that many white Americans and some Black Americans don't have all the details on the period of enslavement. It's not a surprise, because the people in charge of the education system don't seem interested in telling the truth about America being built on enslaved labor and genocide. In the Caribbean, some of the descendants of the colonizers don't like that truth either and want Black people to get over it, which isn't going to happen any time soon.

But the big thing the Caribbean has going for it is that Caribbean historians are exploring our history and writing the history books. This represents a change. In my mother's time, all the history books about the Caribbean were written by white Brits. In my time, there was a mix. We learned more about Caribbean history, and some regional historians were beginning to publish their own books. My daughter has learned more about Caribbean history than she ever wanted to, including the parts where it intersected with British, European, and American history. And she's learned it from Caribbean historians. That wouldn't have happened if we'd stayed in the UK.

5. You Can Delay "The Talk"

Every Black and BIPOC parent knows about the talk. The specifics may vary depending on where you live, but it's all about making sure your child comes out of any interaction with the police free (in the UK) and alive (in the US).

I'd be the last to say our policing is perfect, but in the Caribbean, the color of my skin doesn't predispose me to getting shot. And the fact that many police don't even carry guns helps, too.

That means when you raise your kids in the Caribbean, you don't have to deliver the talk the minute they leave the womb. Instead, you can take a more measured approach. I remember talking to my daughter about avoiding looking like she was shoplifting when she was around 10. But it wasn't till she was heading to the US for school that I gave her the full spiel on how to stay alive, ably captured in an article by Sanya Whittaker Gragg, titled "To My Beautiful Black Sons: Come Home ALIVE."

6. A Better Sense of Self-Worth

Often, when you exist in spaces where you're minoritized, there's a feeling that you're somehow wrong. That can chip away at your self-esteem day in, day out. The microaggressions and outright racism are tiring.

I have less of that to deal with in the Caribbean. It's hard to know how much it matters to live among Black and brown people till you no longer have it. But what it means — and I'm only just putting this into words — is that my sense of self doesn't depend on the white gaze. And that is hugely important to how I carry myself in the world.

Nowhere's perfect, of course. My experience as a dark-skinned Black woman isn't the same as that of my biracial daughter. For some, she's not Black enough; for others, she's too "white." But in spite of how others see her, she's secure in her own identity. And that means that even while doing what she needs to stay safe in the US, she doesn't accept that sense of wrongness. For me, that's priceless, and it means we made the right decision.

11
ANTI-BLACK BIASES – WHY MOST OF US HAVE THEM

One of the insidious side effects of systemic, centuries-old racial discrimination is that it affects how we as Black people feel about ourselves. And it doesn't just happen in places where enslavement was a factor; it happens in post-colonial societies as well.

That's because of the historical attitude that white was right and everything else was lesser. This plays out in a number of ways, but the most pernicious one is colorism. Colorism, also known as shadeism, is discrimination against people based on their skin shade.

In most societies built on enslavement, the closer you were to looking white and European, the closer you were to acceptability. That divide and conquer system started by segregating enslaved persons in terms of the jobs they did. Work in the sugarcane or cotton fields was reserved for those with the darkest skin or those of lighter hue who had fallen from grace. It was the bottom of the social heap or a punishment — take your pick as to which was worse. It's no wonder that to this day, Black people in post-enslavement societies shun agricultural jobs, at least if working for others. That multi-generational trauma runs deep.

The lighter you were, the closer you were to the top of the social scale. In enslaved societies, that status might get you into the house, where you could see further examples of white behavior to mimic. Lighter-skinned enslaved people were encouraged to look down on their darker-skinned peers, even though they were all enslaved. Divide and conquer, again.

No one talked about the fact that lighter-skinned enslaved people resulted from rape, often of young girls. (Ever notice how stories of Thomas Jefferson having a Black "mistress" conveniently leave out her age?)

Still, the products of this assault were held up as the pinnacle of beauty and acceptability within the Black community and were less unacceptable within the white one. How's that for a mind trip?

*

So what does colorism look like in our time? First, let's take a quick look back.

Five generations ago, my ancestors were still enslaved. (If you're American, that generation gap is even smaller.) Let that sink in.

I remember the day I realized that my great-grandmother's parents had been born into slavery. It was mind-blowing. It's not that long ago. The society she was born into valued light skin and white skin. White skin owned practically everything; light skin could have a great position in society.

The physical manifestations of acceptability weren't just limited to skin, though. They included hair — good hair, which was hair that was as close to European and as far away from African in texture as you could get. If you didn't acquire it by birth, you had to achieve it, by dint of hot combs and chemicals. Some went as far as using skin-lightening creams, all in the quest of a whiter shade of pale.

And you can see why — because the light-skinned people got the banking and insurance jobs with the security that meant they could have a confirmed place in society, that they would no longer have to struggle.

Even today, many Black people have a complicated relationship with our skin, our hair, and our very essence. Dark-skinned people like me want to love ourselves, and we often do, but the external narrative doesn't support that self-love. The language of bias pervades everyday interaction, as we talk disparagingly about the darkness of our skin and the nappiness of our hair.

Particularly in white-majority spaces, we also learn that we are unworthy of living, of being, of having good things (whether that's cars, education, or jobs). It tells us we have to struggle, but then mocks our struggle.

Sure, things have gotten better. My parents believed in Black power and raised me and my sister to feel empowered. But even they couldn't fight the messages we got elsewhere in society, the messages that said some of us were more or less worthy because of the color of our skin. Unlearning something so deeply ingrained takes a long time, and the feeling of unworthiness may never go away altogether.

But it is something we have to fight so that the next generation feels better about themselves than our great-grandparents, grandparents, parents, and we, ourselves, did. It's way past time.

WORKING WHILE BLACK

I spent 15 years working in the UK and have experienced firsthand racism in a country where people like me are in the minority. In swapping tales with family members who live and work in the US, I realized that there's a certain universality about the experience of being the only Black person in a white space. This next collection takes a look at that.

12
THE DOUBLE TAKE: INTERVIEWING WHILE BLACK

How the white gaze can seriously hurt your job prospects

If you're Black and you have a name you've inherited from the colonizers, then you've likely seen the double take. It's that moment when you walk into a room and your interviewers realize that, despite your anglicized name, you're actually Black.

The classic double take follows a particular pattern. First, their eyes widen (there may or may not be a stifled gasp). Next, the eyes sort of glaze over while the person deals with the cognitive dissonance of seeing a Black person when they expected a white one. Finally, there's a weak smile, and they get back to business.

The first time it happened to me, I was in my mid-20s. (I'd previously worked in the Caribbean, where my color wasn't an issue — at least not in terms of employability.) A white colleague and I had applied for the same job. We both thought I had the edge because of my years of writing experience. I also matched every point on the job description. For her, the job was a bit of a long shot. Our interviews were on the same day, so we traveled up together and wished each other luck.

But when I stepped into the room, I could almost hear the indrawn breath. I could feel the thinly veiled shock. And I definitely saw the double take. How the heck did someone whose name was Sharon Hurley look like me?

The interviewers recovered, apparently, and the interview proceeded. (Side note: another thing that goes along with the double take is an aura of disbelief about your qualifications and experience, but I'll talk about that another time.)

Going back on the train with my colleague, we compared notes. I'd done a great interview. She said she'd flubbed hers. She was sure I would get the job.

But I didn't. She did and was pretty embarrassed about it.

I wasn't surprised, though, because that double take had sealed my fate. And because we were fortunate enough to be able to compare résumés and experiences, it's one instance where the implicit bias that often harms Black people's career prospects was crystal clear.

Fast-forward a few years, and I had another surreal experience. The CEO of a non-governmental organization had traveled to London to interview me as a potential editor for their journal, newsletter, and books. He liked what he saw and invited me up to see the panel.

When I walked in, an older gentleman asked me why I hadn't applied to work for *The Voice* (a Black-oriented paper in London). I replied that education concerned everyone, and I didn't see why the color of my skin should pigeonhole me. He asked a couple more questions along those lines, and I began to wonder if I even wanted the job. I got it in the end and enjoyed it, but I could never rest easy when I attended meetings where that person was in the room.

Now, you'd think that switching to working mostly online would stop this kind of thing from happening, but it hasn't. The digital double take is alive and well, along with discrimination based on skin color. Racism, really — let's call it what it is.

I no longer have the email, but I remember being offered a writing gig by a South African woman, who was happy with everything right up till she discovered I was Black (probably via my Twitter account). All of a sudden, her well-thought-out content plan became less certain, and we didn't end up working together.

And then there are the people who imply that as a Black woman I shouldn't be charging as much as I do for my services. I'm well educated and have decades of experience, but for some people, that's not enough.

My story isn't unique: every Black person I know who has ever applied for a job has seen the double take at least once.

At some point, I decided to do some digital triage of my own. My photo is on my website and all my social media profiles, so those who see it as a problem can absent themselves. If someone is prepared to ignore my skill because of my skin color, I don't want to work with them anyway.

13
SURPRISE, I'M QUALIFIED!

True stories of how white employers underestimate Black employees' education and ability

For Black people, one of the unwelcome realities of living and working in countries where you're in the minority is that some white people lower their expectations about your education, capability, and achievements.

My first experience of this wasn't in a work setting, though it did relate to a skill I would later use in a professional capacity.

When I lived in France, I shared a flat with a girl from the US Midwest. We had both done BAs in languages, but she could hardly string a sentence together. It blew her mind that a girl from the English-speaking Caribbean could speak French more fluently than she could. And it was even more mind-blowing when I detailed just how rigorous my education in foreign languages had been.

Of course, she wasn't the only one to doubt my ability. When I returned to the Caribbean, I applied for a travel rep job with a major Canadian airline. My interviewer, who was white, didn't believe I could really speak French. (What would be the point of claiming it if I couldn't, I wonder?)

Anyway, I started speaking and she had to beg me to shut up, because my French was more fluent than hers. I didn't get the job, though, which is just as well, as they wanted to police my hair. I talk about that in "Hair So Problematic."

Fast-forward a few years, and I was in the UK, taking part in a job skills course. The white trainer thought I was stupid because I didn't comment on what was going on in the course.

The truth was that I had nothing to say, as the content wasn't new to me, and I didn't want to ruin it for everyone else. There was a test at the end of the day, and when my results came in, my language skills exceeded expectations. He admitted that he'd expected me to fail, which was an eye-opener for me.

Getting back to more recent events, here's another example. One of my relatives in the US was having a watercooler chat about education with her white colleagues. When she mentioned her qualifications, this was the response: "You have a master's?"

Her white colleagues were visibly shocked, dismayed, and almost affronted. How dare this Black woman be more educated than they were? When she shared the story on social media, dozens of her friends came forward with similar stories. It's as if a Black woman with a post-grad degree shakes their worldview. (Not sure how they would cope with the fact that I have two.)

Even before I did my post-grad studies, I worked in an office in the UK where most people were young and had taken the job straight out of high school. For those people, the fact that I had a degree was also surprising, as most of them didn't. I remember having a conversation with my head of department and wondering if I'd always have to listen attentively to people who were far less knowledgeable about the world than I was. News flash: I had to do it for a long, long time.

If low expectations represent one unwelcome reality, a second unwelcome reality is that even though, as a Black professional, you may have the qualifications and experience for a role, there's no guarantee you won't be overlooked in favor of someone less experienced but with a "face that fits" — usually a white face. (I told the story of one such experience in "The Double Take: Interviewing While Black.")

And that applies to being considered for promotions, too. You'd think that having produced good work in the past would give you an edge, but that doesn't always work for Black people.

One of my relatives applied for a promotion within her department after successfully handling a rebranding exercise that got the attention of the CEO. But her immediate boss felt threatened by her and actively took steps to diminish her. In the end, the promotion went to someone far less qualified who was adept at looking like they were working without actually doing much.

Finally, here's a third unwelcome reality: if you're Black and work in an office where you're in the minority, you'll often go through your entire working life frustrated at being overlooked, being bossed around by those less competent than you, and having to deal with racist microaggressions daily.

The irony is that Black people know they often have to be twice or three times as good to merit the same consideration as their white colleagues, so they tend to prioritize education and may often be the most educated and capable people in the room.

Ready to do better? Here are a few suggestions:

If you're hiring people, be aware of your own implicit biases and make sure you look at a good range of résumés.

Be aware of discounting the opinions of Black employees or, even worse, asking them to be the arbiter of everything that relates to diversity.

Do the work: read books, watch programs, listen to podcasts, talk to Black people, and broaden your expectations of what a Black person is or should be.

14
THE LONELINESS OF THE SOLE BLACK EMPLOYEE

True stories of the Black experience in office life

You know the day is coming. You sent in your application, made it through the interview process, and got hired. Now it's time for your first day, and there's one big hurdle you'll have to face, today and every day. You'll be the only Black employee in the company.

When you live in countries where you're in the minority, this is a common experience. You don't see anyone who looks like you on the interview panel, and you sure as heck don't see any in the office or the lunchroom. It's just you — the only Black or brown face in a sea of whiteness — and it's a lonely place to be.

Apart from the loneliness, there's a heavy weight of responsibility, too. You know you're the person everyone in that office will use to judge all Black people, present and future.

Many of them have never interacted day to day with anyone who looks like you. Some will be open-minded and friendly; others will be closed-minded and not so friendly. And there'll probably be a couple of outright racists in there, too.

While inside your home, you're just you, but the minute you leave, your Blackness becomes the first thing that the white majority notices about you. As you commute to work, you may see people shrink away as if you're going to rob them. And you may wait twice as long for a cab as the blond person next to you.

When you get to the office, superficially, everything's OK. But the microaggressions can start as early as your first day. You may have to convince a security guard that you actually work there. Or you'll find that rather than being allowed to make your own way upstairs, someone has to accompany you. (Once you're on the team, it may not happen again, but it's a clear sign of the implicit biases that will affect your working life.)

As you fill in your paperwork, and people make small talk, the microaggressions continue. Surely you can't be from here? Oh, you are? But where are your parents from? If it's not this country, then your questioners can safely put you in the "lesser" box and get on with their day.

Early on in your relationship with the company, you may get questions about your hair. Some co-workers may be rude enough to put their hands in it. And there are other microaggressions, too, about how you speak, about how you write, about your education, about — whatever you do or are that's perceived to be outside the norm for a Black person.

But it's even worse when it comes to doing your actual work. For example, in a meeting, people will often talk over you and ignore you or, even worse, listen and dismiss you. You might be brilliant and have great ideas, but they'll never know because their minds are firmly closed to the possibility that a Black employee might have value to offer.

And that goes double if you're a Black woman. You may find that it takes longer to get projects approved, that there is more micromanagement and oversight, and that if something works well, you might not even get the credit (though you'd better believe you'll get the blame if anything goes wrong).

You can't even be sure that your manager will support you. Often, that manager is threatened by your intelligence and will block you from opportunities for advancement.

But it doesn't get much better when people listen. Because they only tend to listen when it's a question of issues that have to do with Black people.

Suddenly, you're *the* expert on diversity, equity, and inclusion, even if that has nothing to do with your day job. You're *the* expert on the Black experience, even though by now people should know that Black people aren't a monolith.

The Black community is as diverse as any other. The cultures of Black people from the US, the UK, the Caribbean, and the plethora of African countries can and do vary widely, even if we all share a melanated skin shade.

And you can't win: bring up diversity issues outside the allotted discussion slots and you're met with eye rolls and sighs because the Black person is talking about diversity *again.* In some cases, talking too much about inequity can get you fired.

Somehow you struggle through the day, counting the minutes till you get back to your sanctuary, your home. Sadly, you'll have to do it all again tomorrow, and for much of your working life.

It's no wonder you're tired. It's no wonder you've decided to keep your head down, get on with the job, and avoid making race an issue.

*

I've been that person, reserving conversations about racism for late-night confabs with my girlfriends. But lately something's changed. I've been more vocal publicly about racism and related issues since 2020 than I have my whole life.

I've talked to friends and acquaintances and also complete strangers who've responded to my articles and LinkedIn posts.

One of my friends said I was "giving a voice to the voiceless." What they meant by that was that they couldn't speak out in their workplace for fear of repercussions. (You'd better believe that when you interrogate the white patriarchy about diversity, equity, and inclusion, there are repercussions, ranging from side-eyes and snarky remarks all the way up to losing your job.)

But I'm a freelancer, so I can speak, because nobody can fire me. Sure, there may be some jobs I don't get. I'm sure there are people who are uncomfortable with what I've been posting. Hearteningly, there have also been those who are listening and learning and committing to do better.

I plan to continue to highlight these issues where I can and to amplify the voices of those who are leading the way on anti-racist action.

My view is that everybody needs to be talking about this. Let me make it clear to my white friends and colleagues: I don't hate you; I just hate racists.

But hating racists isn't enough. The question is, What are we doing to challenge racist behavior? If you're white, how are you using your white privilege to support your Black friends and colleagues? Are you having hard conversations about racism with the people who look like you?

Because that's what needs to happen next. It will be difficult, challenging, and uncomfortable, but unless we all do it, nothing will change.

15
PARDON, YOUR BIAS IS SHOWING

True stories of racial microaggressions in the workplace

I'm going to let you in on a secret: I didn't learn the term "microaggressions" till decades after I'd already experienced my first one.

Microaggressions don't just happen at work, of course. Black people who live in countries where they are in the minority experience them every day, in every sphere of their lives.

(And, just so you know, post-colonial societies where Black people are in the majority aren't exempt from microaggressions either, but that's a story for another time. I talk about that in *Exploring Shadeism*, a study of colorism in Barbados and the Caribbean.)

Most of my experiences of racial microaggressions happened in the UK, where I lived and worked for 15 years. But they're identical to the experiences of my Black relatives and friends who work in the US.

At first, I was simply perplexed by what I considered stupid questions and asinine comments. But it turned out those questions and comments were all subtle ways of letting me know I didn't belong.

Here are some of the experiences that stood out most for me. Let's start with the questions:

How Did You Get Here?

When I first started working in the UK, a few of my colleagues asked how I'd gotten to England. They knew I'd come from the Caribbean, but they couldn't conceive of island nations like ours having modern transportation technology like planes. A couple of colleagues wondered if I'd traveled on some sort of "banana boat," but if I'd said I'd swum 4,000 miles, I'm sure some of them would have believed me.

What Kind of House Do You Live In?

This sounded like an innocuous question until further conversation revealed that my questioners pictured me living in trees. Seriously, I'm not making this up. This happened to me in the early 1990s.

It's not that trees are necessarily a bad place to hang out. It was the assumption of my inferiority that underlaid that question. Honestly, I was staggered by the level of ignorance this question revealed.

Can I Touch Your Hair?

Some people ask. Others just lean in, and before you know it, they've got their fingers in your hair. That's just rude. Once more, for the people in the back:

Hands off Black people's hair. It is not your exotica or curiosity. We had 400 years of that BS and we're over it, OK?

As if the questions weren't bad enough, there were a couple of statements I heard over and over again during my years working in England, such as …

You're So Articulate/You Speak Such Good English

This is one that's been said to me in many workplaces. The tone is what separates a compliment from a microaggression.

If there's admiration, it's likely genuine. If there's surprise, then there's the underlying assumption that Black people aren't articulate.

There's also an assumption that we come from countries where English isn't the first language. That's true for some people, but the colonizers got around and imposed their language. So there are a bunch of places Black people live where English is the first language. Learn some history, people.

I Don't See Color

This one always makes me think the speaker's living in an alternate reality. I'm a tall Black woman, so I think my color is pretty hard to ignore.

Truth to tell, I wish more people would see my color. Then they would acknowledge the whole of me, instead of denying my history and culture.

A twist on this came when my white American roommate in France told me she thought of me as white. Even today, I struggle to wrap my head around all the biases contained in that simple sentence.

In addition to the bias-filled questions, there are other microaggressive experiences (actually, sometimes there's nothing "micro" about them):

Being a Curiosity

I remember when a colleague told me about the "colored chap" who lived in her village. From her tone, you'd have thought he was another species.

Don't get me wrong; she wasn't being unfriendly. In fact, she was going out of her way to make me feel included, but it had the opposite effect. She knew nothing about him other than the color of his skin.

And having been that lone Black person in other places, I can tell you it's a lonely and uncomfortable place to be sometimes. And it's equally lonely and uncomfortable being the lone Black person in an office where you're dealing with this kind of foolishness every freakin' day!

Not Being Seen as a Professional

Another biggie is when people come into the office where I'm working and assume I am "the help," for want of a better phrase. Just as I've seen the double take in interview settings, I've also seen it when someone's come in for a meeting and realizes the Black person he just walked past dismissively is actually the person he's supposed to be meeting.

Sometimes there's the "whitesplaining," as if I don't have skills, too.

I had a bully of a boss who was prone to this, even though I had more industry experience than he did.

From what's shared using the #BlackintheIvory hashtag on Twitter, there are also stories of how any issue related to Black people is somehow less worthy of study and attention.

Being Passed Over for Promotion

This can be hard to judge, but you get a feeling, don't you? The same way I recognize the double take, I know when I'm being seen as not quite good enough, simply because I'm Black.

Sometimes it's witnessing my white colleagues who don't work as hard as I do get a raise or a better raise than I do.

Sometimes I have to apply twice for the promotion that less-qualified people seem to get as of right.

And sometimes I don't get the promotion at all and am subtly disrespected till I choose to leave.

These are only a few of the experiences I've had at work. There have been many others in other contexts. White friends, this is why your Black colleagues are stressed out, unhappy, and ready for change.

16
BUSINESS TRAVEL WHILE BLACK: WHY I'M NOT A RULE BREAKER

True stories of "random" selection and respectability politics

When I'm traveling as a Black woman, there are certain rules I have to follow. These apply to both business and personal travel. In fact, in terms of my appearance, there's really no difference.

I remember my sister traveling on business a while back and coming to visit me before going on to a trade fair. She was dressed to the nines. When I asked why, she said it was less hassle that way.

Although she didn't want to give into respectability politics, it was the lesser of two evils if the alternative was possibly being held by an immigration officer with more time on their hands than education and common sense.

Her "get through immigration free" uniform included a skirt suit (fitted, but not tight), full face of makeup (done, but not "tarty"), medium heels (feminine, but not flirtatious), "serious" handbag, and "tidy" hair.

If she wore her hair in a relaxer versus braids, that made her journey even easier. If she chose to wear her hair in braids, she made sure that they were pulled back from her face and secured in a bun.

Whenever she dressed in this way, she sailed through airports all over Europe without being stopped or hassled. However, every time she deviated from that dress code, she was "randomly" selected for a check.

To this day, if her clothing is "too casual," or heaven forbid, she wears a head wrap, she gets searched and checked every single time. Would she like to dress more comfortably, especially on long-haul flights? Absolutely. Is it worth the trouble? Not for a second.

I take a similar approach. You'll often hear Black people say that we're held to a higher standard than others, and it's true. When I travel, I look with amazement at the white people who are dressed scruffily, have their feet on tables other people will have to use (that's just nasty), and have no problem being loud and jovial. That's not what it looks like for me as a Black person, especially if I am traveling on business.

Before I travel, I'll double-check all the rules about what size your case has to be and what can be in your carry-on. I can't guarantee that a nod and a wink will get me through if something isn't quite right. I'll make sure all my paperwork is in order. I have a British passport, true, but will the color of my skin lessen its utility? I'm never quite sure.

Then there's my dress. Smart casual is the best way to go, if not business casual. As I shared earlier, my sis used to travel in a coordinated outfit that made it look like she had money.

You will not find me traveling in hoodies and sweatpants, even though those would be far more comfortable. Jeans maybe, but nothing with holes in it. The point is to avoid falling into the stereotype.

On the plane, I'm a quiet and unobtrusive presence. That's my personality, anyway, but I really don't want to have to deal with stares or to help someone unlearn their biases about Black people.

Off the plane, I know there's another hurdle to face: getting through immigration. Here's a sample interaction from the land where I was born.

A common question, which people have asked several times over the years, is "Where are you from?"

If people don't like the answer they get, they may follow up with "Where are you really from?" "Where are your parents from?" or "Where were you born"? These microaggressions happen in the workplace, but they also happen when you travel for business or leisure.

I get it. They're puzzled by someone who doesn't match their worldview. Though there are plenty of people of Caribbean origin with British passports, it still seems to surprise some immigration officers. It's as if they can't see past the color of my skin.

A notable example of this was when I was returning to the UK with a friend. We appeared to be the only two Black women on the plane, so of course, the immigration bods pulled us aside on entry to try to establish what business we had there.

"Where are you from?" they asked.

"England," we said.

"But where are you really from?" they asked.

"Southampton," we said, as that's where we were living at the time.

"But where were you born?" they asked.

"Streatham," I answered. It's part of London.

All of this information was in my British passport, which they were looking at.

Confounded, they eventually let us go on our way.

Honestly, I'm never the one who gets to breeze straight through, smartly dressed or not. Some immigration officer always finds a reason to ask more questions. And it's extremely wearing, you know?

So, it's no wonder I expect the worst when I travel to other countries. When flying into the US, I have the address and phone number of the place I'll be staying at my fingertips. I'm pleasant, but only answer what's asked.

But even after that, the microaggressions continue. I may or may not get a cab easily. And when I arrive at the hotel, people are as likely to assume I'm part of the domestic staff as a guest. (I tell no lies.)

Even when people don't speak, I can see it in their eyes: what is that Black woman doing here? I see it every time I walk about the conference venue, in the eyes of staff and guests alike.

And when they challenge me, I can see the surprise as it turns out I'm actually supposed to be there. It's the same as the double take I get from an all-white interview panel.

To sum up, traveling on business while Black requires me to adopt a particular persona, one that minimizes the appearance of threat and maximizes the appearance of respectability.

It requires me to be aware of people's attitudes and expectations at all times. And it requires me to keep a lid on any annoyance I feel, in order to make the whole process go more smoothly.

Is it any wonder I'm tired?

17
SHOWING UP WITH OUR WHOLE SELVES

Why that's not always an option when working while Black

As a Black person, bringing everything that you are to work is a tough decision. After all, if you're in a country where you're in the minority, what you are isn't seen as a good thing.

Let's face it, even in countries where Black people are in the majority, what you are might not be seen as a good thing.

Hiding part of yourself isn't always a conscious decision. Instead, it happens over many little microaggressive moments.

Internalizing the idea of wrongness can start early, like the first time you go to school and people claim not to be able to understand or pronounce your name. Or when they manage to pronounce it, but other you by commenting on how exotic it is.

White people, hear this: however exotic a name may sound to you, for Black people, certain names are as common as John or Jane. It's culture, not exotica.

When you're in class at college and a topic that relates to Black people (which is every topic, but again, that's another story) comes up, then every eye will swivel to you, as if you're some sort of Oracle of the Black Experience. Take it from me: it's an uncomfortable place to be.

This happened to me in England, where though I could talk with authority about my experiences as a Black woman from the Caribbean, I was *not* an authority on the Black experience in Britain. I had only stories from my parents, who lived there in the 1960s.

Really, I can't win. If I don't fit into common stereotypes about Black people, then I'm not really Black. If I have anything in common with those stereotypes, then that's all I am: a representation of the Black experience, not a whole person.

It's the same in an office setting. Assuming I get past the interview panel and actually get the job, I'm seen as different the day I set foot there. Different, and lesser.

In no situation do I feel free to be all that I am. Instead, I keep quiet, don't make too many waves, and hope I'll survive each day with some of my dignity and self-esteem intact. There are many days when that doesn't happen.

All of those experiences happened off-line, but they inform my online interactions, too. When I started freelancing and working primarily online — having seen the double take, experienced the paternalism of white liberals (even women), and been sexualized and discriminated against in different settings — it made perfect sense to me to let my anglicized name do the talking for me, rather than let my Black skin prevent me from getting the work I needed to help support my family.

A couple of early experiences validated this decision, because there were people who discovered I was Black, then tried to use that as a reason to pay me less. Never mind that when I started freelancing 15 years ago, I already had a solid 15-plus years as a journalist under my belt. They couldn't see past my Black face and lowered their compensation offer accordingly.

Another time, in comparing notes with a fellow writer who was less experienced, I discovered that she was actually earning more.

I can't remember exactly when my approach changed. It's probably when I started writing more about social media and implementing those best practices, which included using a photo. But at some point, I finally decided to put my face out there.

Of course, I still wasn't showing up with my whole self, because I didn't tell people where I was. That's because, for many, being Black and living in Barbados equals not up to the job. I'm not making this up. People have actually said to my face that I must spend a lot of time hanging out on the beach. As anyone who knows me knows, it's actually completely the opposite.

News flash #1: I'm a professional writer with a journalism background, so I work from a home office and respect and meet all my deadlines.

News flash #2: Sand, sea, and laptops don't mix. I'm not going to risk damaging the tools of my trade for the sake of a swim. I can do that when I'm not working.

For a long while, I only interacted with clients by email, so they couldn't hear my hodgepodge of an accent, born of growing up in various Caribbean countries and living in England. And I never showed my face on camera.

There wasn't a single moment that led to that changing. Rather, it was an incremental process. Once I'd posted my photo on my social media profiles, where I was sharing my work, there was no reason not to put it on my website. Once my photo was on my website, there was no reason not to take a video call.

And once I'd participated in a couple of video calls, there was no reason not to share more. So when clients asked where I was based, I started telling them.

Of course, I still frame it carefully, because as a Black professional, you have to be better than the rest to be equal, right? That means highlighting my credentials and experience when I have a call with a new client. I make it clear that I've been writing for big-name companies in the US for 15 years and that I have a background in trade journalism in the UK.

This year, I've taken an additional step by writing more about my actual experiences as a Black woman, online and off-line. A couple of people have mentioned that for a long time, I was the only Black woman they knew writing about marketing. My photo helped them to know that it was possible for someone who looked like them to build a successful career. If for no other reason, I'm glad I did it.

Now, I'm happy that I'm able to share my other experiences, too. I hope they will serve as solidarity and inspiration for my Black and BIPOC colleagues. And I hope my stories will show white people just what their Black colleagues face every day. Who knows? Maybe one day showing up with your whole self as a Black person will no longer be exotic or strange.

18
OH, THE GASLIGHTING

A white person's need for comfort does not negate my experience as a Black woman

Let's get something straight: I recognize racism when I see it.

As Rebecca Stevens Alder pointed out in "I Don't See That I Am Black, You Do," I've had plenty of time to hone those skills.

I've seen the surprise when I walk into an interview room, I've had my qualifications and expertise doubted, I've been offered reduced pay, I've been fetishized, and I've been targeted while traveling.

So let me say it again: I know racism when I see it and when I experience it.

That's why when I read an article on racist phrases to avoid — in which Ono Mergen said, "We know full well when something is racist. Stop questioning us and start challenging the status quo" — I jumped in with the following comment: "So tired of well-meaning people trying to explain away a racist microaggression. When you experience racism regularly, you always recognize it."

Several people took exception to that, but one white man in particular saw my comment about recognizing racism as a statement that he was racist. And truly, it wasn't about him.

(Of course, he tried to make it about him by writing an entire article to support his own claim that he was not racist — which, to be clear, I had never accused him of. I was having a conversation with the author of the piece I'd just read.)

Someone else jumped into the conversation by implying that Black people see racism everywhere.

All I'm going to say here is: we see it where it exists. You can draw your own conclusions about whether that's everywhere or not.

I have to admit, I'm tired of the gaslighting. For some white people, the fact that they were unaware of racist intentions is absolution in their own eyes. However, that's not enough for most Black people.

It's the old issue of intention versus impact. Let's talk about that in relation to parenting. When two kids are throwing a ball to each other, and one accidentally hits the other with it, we teach them to apologize for the impact, even if the intention wasn't there. It should be the same with racism, which is way more serious.

If I, as a Black woman or BIPOC, tell you how your words or actions affect me, that's enough reason to 1) apologize and 2) never do it again.

Gaslighting is not a reasonable response.

I don't want to hear that I imagined it or I can't take a joke or any of the myriad comments that minimize my justified pain.

I don't want to be blamed when I'm actually the victim, and I certainly don't want my tone policed.

I don't want to be asked if I'm sure or told that it's not about race.

I don't need people to play devil's advocate for racists — they've already had it their way for centuries.

I want you to apologize, mean it, and do better.

As I pointed out in my further response to the self-appointed gaslighter: "Nobody gets to police what seems racist to me, how I respond to it, or whether I have the will or energy to educate people who don't get it."

Like most people who identify as Black or BIPOC, I am an expert in racism through decades of lived experience. People who have not experienced racism, and who have benefited from a privileged position in society, don't have the chops to negate that experience.

But here's a suggestion: the next time something a Black person says about racism triggers you, think before you gaslight.

Then ask yourself why you're more bothered about being called a racist than being anti-racist. It could lead to a very interesting conversation with yourself.

19
RACE AND THE FREELANCE WRITER, REVISITED

True stories of the discrimination faced by a Black woman while writing and freelancing

As a Black woman, I don't spend a lot of time agonizing over the "fact of Blackness," as Frantz Fanon called it. Usually, I just get on with my life. That doesn't mean I don't notice when inequalities are present. Sometimes it's hard to identify the motivation of the perpetrator, but the result is usually crystal clear.

Does Black and Quiet Equal Stupid? For Some, It Does

I'll be the first to admit that I don't make it easy for people to read me, especially in face-to-face encounters. I'm an introvert and tend to approach situations by sitting quietly, observing, listening, and taking in what's happening. You'll only hear my voice if I think there's a need.

That counted against me when I attended a job fair in the UK.

During the day, participants did tests to determine their best skills and attributes, so the organizers could suggest suitable job avenues. There were also presentations, though they didn't teach me much.

At the end, there was a one-to-one with a trainer to evaluate your results. During my session, I discovered that for my trainer Black + quiet = stupid. So he was amazed by my off-the-charts scores in English and high scores in other categories.

It was a lesson for me in how institutional racism affects people's perception of events. I knew that from then on, I'd have to be more vocal to make an impact, introvert or not.

The Racial Pay Gap

I won't turn this into a litany of woes, but there have been other incidents. Now that I'm writing mostly online, I don't always know for sure whether race plays a part in the decision to hire me or the amount clients want to pay me. (Let's face it: people could also discriminate because I'm a woman.)

Sometimes I have my suspicions, and sometimes I have them confirmed. For example, in comparing notes with a colleague over a particular writing job, I know I was offered about 20 percent less per article than she was. Our skills and experience matched, so my ethnicity had to be the deciding factor. Though I was able to renegotiate, it was a signal that the racial pay gap is alive and well.

I've actually come across people who are affronted because I have the audacity to charge appropriately for my writing skills and experience. One potential client said to me, "Who do you think you are?" I gave him a short list of the reasons my rates are what they are and moved on. Needless to say, we didn't end up working together.

The Big Decision: Should I Show My Face?

When I first went freelance, after polling my colleagues of color who had had negative experiences, I decided not to include a photograph on my website, just in case people made a snap judgment about hiring me before I got a chance to show my credentials.

Later, I reversed the decision, figuring if people would take one look at my face and decide not to hire me, I was better off without them anyway.

Why Are We Still Talking About This?

The short answer to this question is because racism still affects Black writers.

It annoys me that Black writers and writers of color have to think about this at all.

Honestly, I'm tired of it all.

I believe in equality of opportunity and in having the right to compete on a level playing field. I believe that people's work should be judged on its own merits and the color of your skin should not be a consideration in hiring you for a particular job. (Even being the wrong gender can be a problem.)

In the 21st century, that's just wrong.

That's why, while I may be tired of racism, I'll do my part to raise awareness by writing about my experiences.

20
HAIR SO PROBLEMATIC

True stories of racist hair discrimination

The first time I realized my natural hair could be a problem for others was while attending a Catholic primary school in Trinidad. I was eight, I believe, and Sister R, the nun in charge, called my parents in to ask them to "do something about my hair." I'm not sure what exactly she expected them to do with my exuberant '70s 'fro, but she didn't get the response she was expecting.

Despite the very real possibility (in my young mind) that she could use her hotline to the deity to get us all into trouble, my parents didn't cooperate at all. As I recall, my dad's view was that as long as my hair was clean and neat there was nothing to talk about. It's the only time I'd seen the sister back down. I never heard another word about my hair for the rest of my time at that school.

*

A few years later, we moved to Barbados. I've talked before about the colorism that pervades Barbadian society, so it's no surprise that almost everyone around me wanted to do something about their hair. Decades later, I still recall comments about the "impossibility" of dealing with natural hair and the desirability of straightened hair.

Aside from the hot iron and chemical straighteners, in the '80s, Black women also had the option of the Jheri Curl. This was an oily curly perm that became the butt of many stand-up comics' jokes. Or you could braid your hair in the style co-opted by Bo Derek in *10*. (I say co-opted because women of African ancestry have been styling their hair in elaborate braided patterns for centuries. The irony, of course, was that what was considered cute on a white woman was considered unprofessional on a Black one.)

I wore braids a lot in the mid- to late '80s, but as I later discovered, what was fine for a student was unacceptable in many workplaces. When I was very young, I remember being fascinated by my aunties' weekend hot-ironing ritual to get their hair ready for the work week. As an adult, I learned why they did it.

In one of my job interviews, I was told that if I got the job, I'd have to straighten my hair, because braids weren't allowed. That happened to many women, so it's no surprise that most of them caved and switched to a more "acceptable" hairstyle.

This still happens around the world. People of the global majority have their hairstyles policed by both white people and BIPOC who are operating from the same playbook.

While hair discrimination (which is racism, let's be clear) mostly affects women, Black men aren't exempt from the problem. In the last year alone, we've seen Black children excluded or expelled from school because of their hair and a Black football player having his locs cut off. In fact, you don't have to look very hard to find dozens of similar stories.

It's so bad that people are having to pass legislation like the Creating a Respectful and Open World for Natural Hair (CROWN) Act in the US to stop anti-Black hair discrimination at work.

Let's be clear: the way I wear my hair doesn't affect my ability to do my job. As far as I'm concerned, if my hair is clean and in an appropriate style for my ethnicity, it's nobody's business.

*

Of course, the bias against natural hair isn't just in the workplace; it's out in society. When I was at university and in the early days of my working life, it was clear that white European hair norms were what most guys preferred. When I switched to short natural hair, an ex referred to it dismissively as "man head." And many Black women will attest to the fact that their partners often favor long, straight hair that mimics European hair norms.

With that kind of attitude, it's hard to learn to love your own hair and your own self. Everything about society tells you that what you are is not right — and not close enough to white.

In the past, it always seemed that my preference for natural hair was a bit shameful. Though I've worn short natural hair regularly over the years, and exclusively in the last seven or so, it's taken me decades to be unapologetic about it. I think all women should have the right to choose their hairstyle and outlawing Black hairstyles at work or school is just plain wrong.

*

If they *do* wear their hair natural, or in an elaborate style, Black women face another problem: the number of white people who want to stick their hands in it and feel it for themselves. White people, I beg you, resist the temptation. You are awakening centuries of generational trauma caused by not having agency over our own bodies, by being seen as less than people, by being curiosities at best. Keep your hands out of my hair; it is not your plaything.

Also, accept that many of us like to do things with our hair. (I'm the exception, as I truly can't be bothered.) But when you see a Black woman who has a different hairstyle from the day before, it's not an invitation to quiz her about whether it's hers ("If I bought it, I own it," as one friend says blithely) or how the style was achieved. Say, "I love your new hairstyle," and move on. Trust me, we do not want to spend 15 minutes giving you a Black hair tutorial at work. If you're that curious, Google it.

Minoritized people are tired of our hair being either a problem or a curiosity for white employers and white society. Flip the script: if a white woman went to a Black-majority country and couldn't get certain jobs because of her natural hair and had to somehow make it into something that resembled Black natural hair, we'd think it was ridiculous, wouldn't we? That's because it is.

Time for racist hair discrimination to end.

21
SEEN YET UNSEEN

How Black people's individuality is often ignored

Ask any Black person who's worked in a white-majority country, and they'll probably have experienced what I'm about to describe at least once. It's happened to me dozens of times.

I've talked before about the loneliness of being the only Black employee. That can be rough, but there's another hurtful thing that happens when you're *not* the only one.

At its simplest, it looks like a case of mistaken identity: when a white colleague addresses me by the name of the other — or another — Black employee in the office. And maybe if it happened once, I'd buy it.

But if it happens multiple times and it's people I work with every day, then it begins to look like they can't be bothered to tell us apart. There's underlying racism in seeing all Black people as a homogeneous and interchangeable group. Plus — take it from someone who's been on the receiving end — it just doesn't feel good.

If you consistently mistake me — or misname me — for a shorter, lighter-skinned Black colleague, it's going to hurt me, a tall, dark-skinned Black woman. Sure, some people look alike, but if mine is a face you're seeing every week, and sometimes every day, there's no excuse.

And, let's be clear, even if the other Black person in the group is also tall and dark-skinned, she's unlikely to look like me. I think I'd know by now if I had an identical twin. If people really looked beyond the immediacy of skin color, they'd find that many of our features are different.

In another iteration of this, the white person is convinced I must be related to the only other Black person they know. And when I deny it, they refuse to take my word for it. Again, this has happened to me several times.

Yes, I say, mentally rolling my eyes, *I'm sure I'm not related to some random Black person you know*. If I start to unpack it, I'll usually find that this other Black person is from a different country, has a different accent than I do, and may even have a different skin tone. In other words, we look nothing alike, and there's no possibility we could be related.

The sting in the tail of this particular experience is that Black people — and Black women — are often the last to be believed and trusted in any given situation. I can't begin to imagine what my enslaved ancestors went through, but the legacy of disbelief, distrust, and disempowerment is like a skewer through the heart. Please, start believing Black people, and especially Black women.

These cases of mistaken identity don't just happen in the office, of course. The media is full of examples of instances where a story about one Black person featured the image of another. Again, the two people don't usually look alike to anyone who takes the time to look properly. And the hasty apology and fixing of the error does nothing to diminish the outrage and hurt Black people feel when this happens yet again.

Of course, there's a sinister side to this "identity crisis," particularly if you are a Black person living in the US. Being "mistaken" for someone who's committed a crime could literally get you killed. We already have plenty of examples of cases where the person who ended up dead didn't look like — or match the particulars of — the person the police were actually looking for.

Look, I can be pretty bad at names and faces. I've mistaken one person for another plenty of times, especially famous actors who take similar kinds of roles. But the differences are:

1) I don't make the same mistake repeatedly. If someone says, no, that's not who I am, I will apologize and go out of my way to avoid doing that to them again. Repeating the error is just rude.

2) If someone says they're not related to someone I know, I don't ask if they're sure. I assume they know who they are, and who they're related to, and apologize for my mistake.

3) I don't automatically disbelieve what the other person is telling me or refuse to see that person as an individual.

For me, as for many Black people, it's like my white colleagues see me when they want to point out how different or alien I am, but then they don't see me, because they think all Black people look alike. Take it from me, Black people in this position feel disrespected, disempowered, and, if it's happened often enough, angry (though, of course, they can't show it because that plays into another stereotype that seriously hurts their chances of remaining employed).

So as one of the "good white folks," to again steal Marley K's term, what can you do?

If you're working in an office with multiple colleagues who are Black, Indigenous, and people of color, get to know them as individuals.

Learn to distinguish them from one another, and help your less "woke" white colleagues to do the same.

Help your Black colleagues feel seen and valued as individuals, because that makes it harder for outdated racist attitudes to flourish in your work space.

Make the unseen seen, and help end racism in your workplace.

22
BUILDING A BUSINESS WHILE BLACK – IT'S NOT SO EASY

Without generational wealth, the foundation can be shaky

One of my friends asked, "Why is it so hard for Black people to build businesses?" My immediate answer: **the lack of generational wealth.**

I'm not saying there aren't Black people who are rich, and even super-rich, but they are the exceptions rather than the rule. A *Business Insider* report on the *Forbes* World's Billionaires List shows that only seven of the 614 billionaires in the US are Black (and you can probably guess who's on that list).

It has been widely reported that the wealth gap between Black and white families is large. The median white family is $152,000 wealthier than the median Black family, and the median wealth of Black families hasn't grown much since 1992. In other words, the wealth gap is widening.

There are lots of reasons why this can happen. A cartoon I saw a while back shows the stark differences between how Black and white people grow up in the US (and not just in the US, as you'll see). This has a huge effect on both their personal wealth and their ability to access alternative sources of funding.

Another instructive example is David Horsey's 2014 cartoon showing how Black and white people progress toward the American Dream.

It shows how few systemic obstacles there are to white people's advancement and how many systemic obstacles there are for Black people. And it shows that some of the biggest systemic drivers of white people's progress have been the same factors that impeded Black people from progressing (yes, I'm talking about enslavement).

We know that Black kids are more likely to be excluded or expelled from school than their white peers, and we know about the school-to-prison pipeline.

Once Black kids have been stigmatized as troublemakers, the opportunities available to them continue to shrink. This makes it less likely that they'll attend a "good" college or be able to easily start a business.

If they manage to avoid the school-to-prison pipeline and make it to college, many Black students will still have a different experience than their white peers.

Because of that wealth gap I mentioned earlier, BIPOC students have no generational wealth to fall back on and may have to take out loans and get jobs. It's no wonder that Black people also graduate at a lower rate than their white peers.

Those who remain in the system still have to maintain a 4.0 grade point average, because they have to be better than the best to succeed. That's because whether you're talking about education, the workplace, or the launching of a business, many people are ready to believe the worst of BIPOC. That attitude is racism and another factor that makes life harder.

Sure, some white students also struggle, but the stats show that Black students leave college with more debt than white students.

When it comes to starting a business, some Black people may not have personal wealth, let alone generational wealth. Yes, there are exceptions (Madam C.J. Walker springs to mind). But most Black people in the US didn't have the chance to start to amass meaningful wealth until the 1960s. Meanwhile, their white peers had a head start of a couple of centuries, thanks to Black people's enslaved labor. Just let that sit with you for a while.

No matter what the color of your skin is, banks don't think someone who's carrying a lot of debt is a good risk. And remember, Black students typically have higher debt than their white peers. So you can imagine how much more difficult it is for a Black business to get financed. And in a capitalist system, the inability to access funding also limits business growth.

That's without even considering the issue of whether a Black face "fits" or whether lenders are predisposed to apply harsher criteria to Black people. It happens in so many other situations that I wouldn't be surprised. In other words, it looks like we're all running the same race, but BIPOC are starting with a 10-ton weight on their ankles.

Sometimes Black people seek a white partner to circumvent the system. The white face makes it easier for them to access financing and therefore makes it more likely their business will succeed. That just goes to show how deep the racist "white is right" attitude can go.

These differing experiences for Black and white people aren't unique to the US. In the post-colonial society where I live, most of the wealth belongs to the descendants of the enslavers. Their kids get the chance to have summer jobs in family-owned businesses. They can choose where they want to attend college, even if it's thousands of miles away. And they'll graduate without owing a cent, then return to a safe job in another business owned by the family.

Some white people in this situation don't even bother with college, because they don't have to. They know that nepotism will ensure that they outrank and out-earn Black people with PhDs and MBAs.

That's not the experience of most Black people. For some Black people, the norm is to struggle a little to provide opportunities for their children. There's a lot of juggling of priorities to make sure everything is paid for. And some kids don't get the option of living abroad. (I don't want to give a false picture. There are many who manage it, but they all talk about the financial hit. And some have to get into debt to ensure their children will be debt-free.)

Similarly, many Black-owned businesses have to operate without the type of financial safety net most white-owned businesses take for granted. They can't guarantee that if business slows and they have to miss a payment or two, they'll still have a business in a few months' time. Black business owners just don't get the same kind of grace. And they're likely to get even less in the current economic climate.

Yeah, building a business while Black can be hard.

EXISTING WHILE BLACK

Of course, Black people aren't just Black in the workplace. We wear our skin always, and sometimes it affects our experiences, especially abroad. The next section looks at some of those.

23
PAPER CUTS STILL MAKE YOU BLEED

A day in the life of a Black person dealing with racism

I've been mulling over the term "microaggressions" — those racist interactions that most Black people endure, especially in countries where we've been minoritized. I get that we have to call them something, but in some ways, the term minimizes the harm done.

There's nothing "micro" about the way those aggressions make Black people feel. The people who are perpetrating them may not mean to hurt us, but the impact is what matters here, not their intention.

Someone else has called them "death by a thousand paper cuts." Paper cuts hurt as much as any other kind of cut, and paper cuts still make you bleed.

Want to see what I mean? Here's a typical day in the life of a Black person.

*

You wake up. It's a workday, so you get moving and complete your ablutions.

If you're a woman, how will you wear your hair? It kinds of depends on the hair policy at work. Twist outs, braids, or an exuberant afro? If the latter, it's a sure bet some white colleague will have their hands in it before you can say no. Or will you play it safe and go for relaxed, short and natural, or just a wig? Decisions, decisions.

You switch on the news while you get breakfast. Another Black man has died at the hands of the police. It's not a good start to the day.

You scan your cupboard. Cereal, pancakes with syrup, fruit? There's nobody on the packaging who represents your reality. Aunt Jemima doesn't count.

Time to get dressed — conservative is best, especially for women. If you're wearing stockings, you thank your lucky stars that at last you can get a nude that matches your skin and isn't some sort of pale salmon color.

More decisions as you head to work. If you take your car, especially if it's a nice one, and especially if you're a man, you might be stopped, searched, or questioned, as if you don't also have the right to drive an expensive car. And if you're a Black man, there's the ever-present fear that the next police stop may be your last.

Maybe you decide to take public transport. If you're a woman on the subway, you know you risk getting groped. That's not exclusive to you as a Black woman, but your skin color means they grope with more entitlement. At least if you take the train or bus, the seat next to you will be the last to be taken, giving you a much-needed respite. (I've seen people who were dead on their feet stand rather than sit next to me.)

You arrive at the office, and a new security guard is on duty. That means that, yet again, you have to prove you actually work here. Is this the day your white colleagues will support you openly, or will they whisper to you afterwards about how awful it was? Racism has to be challenged loudly in those circumstances for any anti-racist effort to count.

There's a meeting today, so there are some new faces in the office. One of them asks you to get the coffee. You pretend not to hear and head to your desk. You are early, as you know being even a minute late will damn you and all Black people forever. Your white colleague breezes in 30 minutes late with no repercussions. And you know that she'll probably get the next promotion going, even though you're more accomplished and experienced. In spite of your excellent work, you've already been passed over twice, and you'll have to leave if you want to progress in your career.

As you head into the meeting, and set up your presentation materials at the front of the room, someone does a double take when they realize you're presenting. It's not the first time you've seen it, and it won't be the last.

It's time for lunch. Most days, you'll probably eat alone, unless there's a work thing. Those can be tough, because you have nothing in common with your colleagues but work, and you don't want to have to deal with microaggressions at lunch, too.

At lunch, you head to the grocery store to check out some items, but seeing the security guard clock you as a potential shoplifter, you decide you can't be bothered. You enter a clothing store, only to have the shop assistant imply you can't afford to buy anything. Clearly, today is not a good shopping day.

Back to the office for an afternoon meeting. There are more new people, and someone decides to ask where you're from, really? Sigh. Not again. In a casual pre-meeting chat with someone else, he expresses surprise at your post-grad qualifications. The meeting continues. You contribute some ideas, which are ignored till one of your white colleagues says exactly the same thing. Honestly, you can't wait for this day to be over.

You head home and think about going for a jog. These days, that's pretty dangerous, especially if you're a Black man, so you hit the treadmill.

Then you remember there was a loose board on one of your windows. You step outside to fix it. Next thing you know, the police are accusing you of trying to break into your own house. Turns out your white neighbor's visiting auntie called them to say she'd seen a suspicious person. At least this time, you avoid having to go to the station.

You head inside for something to eat. You can't face Uncle Ben tonight, so maybe you'll just order a pizza. Time to relax with some TV. As you skim the channels, you see that another Black woman has died at the hands of the police. You can't bear the minute examination of whether incidents from her past meant she deserved to die, so you keep skimming.

You try to find a program with people who look like you, but there's not a lot to choose from if you don't want to see thugs, criminals, mammies, or people of color who need white people to save them.

Exhausted, you head to bed, knowing you'll have to do this all over again tomorrow.

*

Not everything here will happen to a Black person all in one day, though it's possible. In a week, though, all of them could and probably will. Multiply that by the number of days in a year , and you can see why Black people are tired, why our souls have been bleeding for centuries, and why racism has to end.

24
BLACK WOMEN, STEREOTYPES, AND FETISHES

How the white gaze can endanger Black women

The first time I was racially profiled as a sex worker, I wasn't even fully aware of it. Well, not until later.

I had been working as a teaching assistant in France, and I was heading back home after a party. Although it was around 8 p.m., the September evening was still bright.

As I walked along, mentally reliving moments from earlier in the day, I noticed a car out of the corner of my eye.

Nothing unusual about a car on a street, right? Not usually, but this particular car was driving especially slowly.

I thought it was odd and dismissed it from my thoughts. After all, all my friends were students, and none of us had cars. It seemed unlikely that this weird behavior had anything to do with me.

But it did.

As I got closer to the school building I lived in, the car pulled up beside me. The car window opened, and the driver invited me to get in.

I declined.

He tried to persuade me.

I continued to refuse.

He rolled up the window in a huff and continued to follow me slowly until I turned into the school gates.

It wasn't till much later that I realized he'd thought I was a sex worker off my usual path.

After all, I was in a school zone. Other people were on the streets. So why did he pick on me and nobody else? I can only conclude it was because I was Black. I've since discovered that another Black woman had a similar experience.

The white gaze affects both how we see ourselves and how others see us, and what white people see can put Black people in danger. When a white person calls the police on a Black person, that person can end up dead, though that's not the issue I'm talking about here.

Instead, let's talk about sex. When it comes to sexuality, Black women are often tainted (and fetishized) by the Jezebel stereotype, which goes back to the earliest days of enslavement.

Under the Jezebel stereotype, white people — and white men, in particular — see Black women as hypersexual and always sexually available. It's a particular form of misogynoir that, in extreme cases, can result in women's deaths. Learn more about this in Sope Lartey's "The Jezebel Sticker."

So this white guy saw me walking along the street, minding my own business, and immediately jumped to conclusions.

*

Without a doubt, the Jezebel stereotype was the reason the boyfriend of a French friend propositioned me. He was giving me a ride home, which wasn't unusual, and he said he needed to pick something up at home on the way.

No biggie. I sat in the kitchen's bar area and waited for him to get whatever it was. But when he emerged from the depths of the house, he had a proposition for me.

"I've tried Chinese, I've tried Indian, but I've never tried Black — how about it?"

I was appalled on many levels. First, this was my friend's boyfriend, so even if I had thought of him that way (and believe me, I didn't), he would have been off-limits.

Second, I realized that he had bought into the stereotype about Black sexuality and wanted to test it for himself. I felt like an item on a sexual checklist, rather than an individual.

The third unwelcome realization came after I asked about his girlfriend. His response: "This won't change anything." In other words, sleeping with me would be a novelty, nothing more, and my feelings weren't important.

That represented two stereotypes for the price of one. Black people are often deemed to feel less pain, physically *and* emotionally, so it never occurred to him that this would bother me.

I declined firmly, and he said he would take me home. Then he asked me not to mention it to his girlfriend. I wasn't playing that game, but he needn't have worried. After all, who's going to believe the Black woman's version of events?

We spoke, she cried a little, and in our last phone call, she began some serious gaslighting. She doubted my version of events and his motivations. Later, she resumed her relationship with him as if nothing had happened. Needless to say, that was the end of our friendship.

*

Years later, in Southampton, England, while I was working as a journalist, I had a couple more experiences of being profiled as a sex worker. A friend and I had gone to a scrapyard in search of replacement parts for an old car.

The scrapyard owner looked us up and down in what I now recall as an over-friendly manner and asked if we were working girls.

I was just about to reply in the affirmative (after all, we both had jobs) when, luckily, my friend chimed in. It later turned out that in Brit-speak "working girls" meant sex workers. She knew what he was implying and nipped that idea in the bud.

I shudder to think what would have happened if I had given the answer that I had planned.

*

A few months later, it happened again. On my way to the pub to meet some English friends, a man (of Indian origin) stopped me and implied that he had seen me on a street corner recently. He was pretty insistent, too, but I made my denials and backed off.

Side note: my white English friends asked me at the time why I hadn't just hit him. I pointed out to them that that could have landed me in jail.

The Black woman is never the first person people believe — indeed, she's often the last.

Second side note: it's common to blame the woman for attracting the wrong attention, especially in cases of rape or sexual assault. Though these interactions never got to that level — and that's the wrong approach anyway — let me just say that as a Caribbean woman in a cold climate, I was completely covered, because I was cold. No flesh was on display. Not that that would have been a reason to make assumptions, but … just sayin'.

*

Of course, these aren't the only stereotypes that affect Black people. When you live in places where you're in the minority, you're often surprised by how low an opinion people have of you. Here are just a few examples.

My white landlady in France said she'd never have rented to me if she'd realized in advance I was Black (never mind that the rent was always paid on time and her place was spotless; I have my white roommate to thank for not being evicted, I guess).

My upstairs neighbor in Southampton was surprised that two Black girls didn't make a lot of noise. She was convinced that all Black people played loud music and had wild parties.

Some people assumed I was stupid and talked about me in their own language, not realizing that I understood (this happened to me with French-, Spanish-, and German-speaking people; my German may be rusty, but I know what the word "Black" is).

Multiple people figured a Black woman they couldn't easily pigeonhole had to be a student (in other words, not from here) or nurse (temporarily allowed to be here).

It often blew people's minds when I told them that I was working as a journalist, editor, or university lecturer.

When you're Black, people constantly make assumptions about your upbringing, your education, your work experience — everything about you.

As I've said before, in a workplace setting, they often assume that you're in a junior or domestic role.

So what's the takeaway? I learned that how many white men see me has little to do with me and everything to do with the view that Black women are up for anything sexually. I also learned that it pays to be aware of this view in all my interactions, so I don't end up raped or worse.

Here's what I'd like to happen. I want white people to start seeing Black people as individuals and not some sort of highly sexualized or threatening racial composite.

I want white people to move beyond the biases that we all have and stop putting Black people in uncomfortable, untenable, and, frankly, dangerous boxes. Anti-Black racism isn't just wrong; as we've seen time and again, it can get people killed.

What should you do next?

First, educate yourself. Start with information from Gloria Atanmo about the death by a thousand cuts of systemic racism.

I recommend you follow her on Instagram and read all her posts. They're a good starting point for information about racism and anti-racism.

Second, do the work. Work through an anti-racist reading list (Google it; there are several) so that maybe the next generation of Black women won't be endangered by these same stereotypes.

25
ARE WE BEING SERVED? EATING OUT WHILE BLACK

True stories of racism when eating out around the world

There's a long list of innocuous things Black people do that can trigger racist behavior from white people. You can add eating out to that list. For my white friends, it's a simple matter to grab a sandwich, visit a café or pub, or sit down in a restaurant. If you're a Black person living and working in a place where you're minoritized, it can be anything but. I've got a few personal stories to share that illustrate my point.

Are We Being Served?

Let's start with my trip to Uzès in the late '80s. It's a small town (closer to a village, really) in the south of France. A German friend and I stopped there, hoping to grab a bite before continuing our local sightseeing tour. We saw a café with outdoor seating in a courtyard in a cobbled street. It seemed perfect for the late spring day.

There were a couple of people waiting to be served, so we sat down to wait our turn. As we sat, I saw a couple of funny looks, but I attributed them to locals being surprised at the presence of strangers in "their" spot. While we waited, we chatted, and chatted, and chatted, till we realized we'd already been there for almost an hour without being served.

We caught the waiter's eye and beckoned him over. He looked at us and appeared to acknowledge that we were requesting his presence, but he never actually showed up. My white friend was puzzled, but I knew what was happening. They didn't want to serve Black people. She was indignant and wanted to confront him, but I was happy just to leave. I didn't think making a fuss would get us anywhere.

That was the first time that happened to me in France, but it wouldn't be the last, and I had similar experiences in other European cities.

It's All About the Optics

Some racists aren't quite as obvious as that French waiter. They'll let you in, but you can tell they don't really want you there. You know how when you go to a restaurant, and if they're trying to make it look busy, they'll put new people that walk in near the window, where passersby can see them? It's a common tactic, according to my friends in the hospitality industry.

But if you're Black, you won't always be seated near the window. A few years ago, my sister and I wanted to eat at an Italian restaurant in New York. It was pretty empty, so we figured we'd get a table with a view of the street. But no. They seated us right down in the back, where nobody could see us. We weren't quite sitting next to the restroom, but close. A few minutes later, a white couple came in, and they got a seat near the front. Spot the difference.

Of course, what we should have done was leave, but we'd been walking all morning and we were hungry. So we mentally rolled our eyes and took the table we were offered. While the food was good, the service was shoddy, as if they couldn't be bothered to put in any effort. We both agreed that we'd never go there again.

A Tale of Two Restaurants

Sometimes the racism is even more blatant. The year is 2018. Picture two restaurants within a few yards of each other. One of them is empty; the other is bustling. Three Black women come to the door of the empty one. Admittedly, we don't have a reservation, but there is literally nobody in the place.

Do they offer us a table? Do they heck! They claim that all their tables are reserved, so we move on to the place next door. That restaurant is bustling, but they don't let that be an issue. They ask us to wait a couple of minutes while they organize something. They find us a table, and we're soon enjoying a delicious meal.

How do I know the first situation had to be racially motivated? Because when we walked past on our way home after our meal, the first place still wasn't full, and the maître d' couldn't look us in the eye.

*

These are just a few of the instances that happen when you try to go to a nice place to eat as a Black woman. Depending on the location and the mood of the staff, they may assume you're a sex worker looking for trade or that you can't actually afford to eat there. All of that affects whether you actually make it through the door.

What Happens When You Get a Seat at the Table

If restaurant staff *do* let you in, they may try to rush you through your meal. Ostensibly, it looks like super-fast service, but if you've been through it before, you know they just don't want you there. I've had people bring the bill before offering me dessert, whisking away drinks I haven't quite finished.

It's even more noticeable when I'm in a group of mixed ethnicities, and the standard of service I receive is sometimes noticeably worse. That can mean staff assuming I don't understand the menu, being served last, or having inexplicable problems with my order. Admittedly, poor service can happen to anyone, but it's a pattern that's been repeated with Black people many, many, times.

In those groups, there are also other issues to deal with. Dinner table conversations can be fraught with microaggressions. The double take from people who weren't expecting a Black person to turn up at the table. The questions about where you're really from. The surprise that you've traveled, studied, or excelled in your profession.

Granted, these experiences don't happen every time I eat out or everywhere I go, but every Black person I know has a couple of stories similar to these, so they happen often enough for it to be a problem. The bottom line: for Black people, eating out isn't always a simple matter of picking the nearest place and walking in. You're always aware that racism may rear its ugly head, and you may have to put on your mental armor before walking in, if you get in at all.

26
WHY THIS MAN'S DAUGHTER IS SCARED TO VISIT AMERICA

And why it's more important than ever to speak up about inequity

"I don't want to visit somewhere where I can get shot for doing nothing," said my dual-heritage daughter, when we were discussing a possible trip to the US. Unspoken were the words "because I look Black." I would have loved to tell her she was wrong, but I couldn't.

For a long time I didn't talk or write about race much. And it's not because I don't care. I do, almost too much. But sometimes I don't want to discuss it anymore. And sometimes I can't believe that we still have to think about these issues, much less talk about them. But the conversation with my daughter made me think it was time to break my silence.

Lately, every other day it seems there's news of the shooting of an unarmed Black male (and occasionally a female). Later, he usually turns out to be innocent. Even for those whose reputations aren't squeaky clean, the "reach for the gun" approach favored by many US cops seems excessive and downright crazy to those of us looking on from the outside.

I'm British-born and Caribbean raised and have divided my adult life between the two cultures. In both Barbados and the UK, where most police aren't armed, the police culture in the US — and the gun culture in general — leaves us puzzled, particularly in the wake of so many studies that say that when you get rid of the guns, fewer people are shot.

Makes sense, right?

I'm all in favor of freedom. My ancestors marched, fought, and died for their right to be seen as equal. But when one person's freedom impinges on another person's right to live without fear, something is wrong.

But the question of race is bigger than the issue of who's most likely to get shot. It's about systemic discrimination and oppression of the rights of one group over another.

Even in the UK, where getting shot for no reason is less of a problem for people of color, there are still issues to contend with. Black people are more vulnerable to stop and search requests, and as in the US, Black males form a disproportionate amount of the prison population, relative to their demographic presence.

In both countries, some of the best-intentioned people are also the most clueless, wanting to hope that things are better than ever for people of color. After all, don't we have equality legislation in place?

Legislation is a good start, but it doesn't stop discrimination.

I've had my share of racial discrimination, across more than 40 years and several countries. Some incidents that stand out include

- Pointing, staring, and whispering in France
- Evaporating accommodation in London
- Being denied entry to a restaurant in New York

- Losing out on jobs for which I was clearly better qualified (I happened to know one of the other candidates and we discussed this.)

Yes, on both sides of the Atlantic, some of us still have to work twice as hard to be considered half as good.

And I haven't even had it bad. Among my Black friends, almost all can tell of similar or worse experiences.

Sure, some things have improved, but our condition is a long way away from being perfect.

For Black people, everything you do is under scrutiny, and actions of other ethnicities that pass without comment somehow become a reason to tear you down. As we've seen with Gabby Douglas and Simone Biles, you could win Olympic gold for your country and still be criticized.

Even away from those dizzying heights, people will still question your choices. I've had well-meaning liberals offer their views on race as though I should applaud them, while simultaneously uttering vacuous comments about my name, choice of residence, background, and education. I've been the victim of other people's assumptions, positive and negative.

The partial antidote to this is something all people of color have to learn: how to present yourself in a certain way to make white people feel comfortable with you. We all know the unwritten rules about how you must appear and behave to avoid attracting negative attention, and we teach those to our children to protect them, while resenting the need to do so.

That still doesn't always stop incidents from happening, especially in the US, where it seems that trigger-happy individuals somehow have the right to shoot first and ask questions later, especially if your skin is the "wrong" shade.

To my daughter and many others like her, racism doesn't make sense. Discrimination on the basis of ethnicity is, quite simply, silly. But she reads the news and knows that that conviction won't save her if she happens to be in the wrong place at the wrong time.

That's why I can't blame her for feeling afraid of visiting America when there are so many instances of a huge disparity in the response to perceived wrongdoing depending on the color of your skin, and where the "shoot first and ask later" policy seemingly operated by many law enforcement officers puts her life at risk if she's there. Sure, she's a teenager, but she knows that in the US teen and tween boys are gunned down. So it's not just adults who are at risk.

I'd love to be able to tell her she's wrong and she will be safe, but I can't, because we're not there yet and who knows if we ever will be. Instead, I pass down the knowledge of how to be invisible — or at least acceptable — so no one ever has to add her name to that long list of people shot in America. I don't want to see her or anyone else I know in the headlines for the wrong reasons. There are plenty of other places in the world where Black people are less likely to be shot. Maybe it's time to visit some of those.

In the meantime, here's my message to everyone who cares about this: let's keep talking, writing, and making videos. Let's keep highlighting inequality. Let's shout loudly when someone gets it wrong — and when they get it right. Only when we are *all* willing to engage with issues of race, whatever our own ethnicity, will we have a hope of putting it right[2].

---

[2] Well after publication of this essay, my daughter spent two years at college in the US. In the end she chose to transfer her studies to the UK. Though there are issues there, too, she felt she would be much safer.

27
THE BATTLE FOR REPRESENTATION STARTS IN CHILDHOOD

How unseen Black kids become unseen Black adults

When you start talking about diversity, you'll often hear people say that representation matters. If you're in a work setting, you might think that means having more diversity in the boardroom, but that's not the only place it matters.

In fact, the problem of non-representation of Black people starts way earlier, in childhood. Let's take a look at some typical experiences for Black children.

What Color Is "Flesh"?

When white kids get a cut, they take for granted that they'll be able to patch it up with a "skin" or "flesh" colored bandage. Until very recently — and I'm talking within the last couple of years — that wasn't true for Black people.

All through my childhood, I had pink plasters (they weren't skin to me, no matter how they were labeled) or fabric plasters in a weird shade of salmon. As the genre expanded, I could get different shades of flesh, none of which matched my own. Though I didn't label it as such then, the realization that my skin wasn't seen as "skin" led to moments of cognitive dissonance.

Do Your Dolls Look Like You?

It's not so bad now, but in my own childhood in the Caribbean, having a Black doll was a rarity. My parents went all out to make sure we had several (we still wanted Barbies, too, to be honest). All the dolls we saw on TV looked like white girls or women. For us, those were dolls, and what we had were Black dolls.

Though I'm glad now that my parents took that stance, I don't think my sister and I appreciated the Black dolls as much as we might have. Most little girls (I was an exception) like doing their dolls' hair. Good luck doing that with the Black dolls of the '70s and '80s. Those dolls definitely reinforced the idea that Black hair was difficult to manage, so what did that mean for us?

I didn't see a Black Barbie (complete with Eurocentric hair) till the '90s. They may have existed before, but I was no longer playing with dolls.

My own daughter had dolls of all hues, with a variety of hair types, and we even found one that looked a little like her. Progress, indeed. But for her as well, most of the must-have dolls she saw advertised looked like white girls or women. You see the problem, don't you? If dolls are beautiful, and they don't look like you, then maybe you aren't beautiful.

Dancing Around the Color of Skin

I never took ballet lessons, but the default uniform is pink from head to toe, and professionals wear tights that blend with white skin. That doesn't work so well if your skin is dark, and it's a reminder that as a Black person you're not the norm.

My daughter had this issue when she took dance lessons, and it sometimes felt like her skin and curly hair were a problem when it came to costuming.

Thankfully, that's changing a little. I read not long ago about the prima ballerina who cried when she was finally allowed to wear brown underpinnings for her ballet costume. It's taken way too long to get there, in my opinion.

Is Black Beautiful?

Let's talk about teen mags and beauty mags. By now, you know where I'm going with this. These days, it's a little more common to see a Black face on the cover of a mainstream magazine. Sometimes you'll even see more than one.

That's a relatively recent development in Black history. I don't remember seeing any such magazine covers when I was growing up, and even into my 20s, it was rare, apart from the occasional supermodel. Again, the message is: Black is not beautiful. Even if your parents tell you that you are, it's hard to deny the evidence of your eyes.

Are You in the Story?

I grew up on Enid Blyton's books, Nancy Drew, Hardy Boys, and a whole host of classic children's stories, old and new. Later, I branched out to sci-fi, thrillers, romance, and more. In most of those books, there were no Black characters (at least none that I recognized), and certainly no Black characters in major roles. I didn't think about it; it was just how it was.

Just the other day, I was reading a book when it suddenly occurred to me that the heroine was Black. Even though there are more and more Black writers, that's still rare enough for me to have mentally noted it. After all, if we write what we know and we grow up in white-majority countries and our influences are white writers, then there's a fair chance we might end up with supporting roles in our own stories. Kudos to those who actively fight that.

The Few Black People on TV

The vast majority of the TV shows I watched growing up had no Black characters. *Star Trek*'s Lieutenant Uhura was a welcome exception (and she was a woman, too, which completely delighted me).

Once Black, Indigenous, Latinx, and other POC characters started filtering into my consciousness, I noticed that there was still a representation problem. Some were played by white people in blackface or other makeup. Many of those who weren't fell into the well-worn stereotypes about Black people. I won't dignify those by listing them here, but suffice it to say I wasn't represented.

Later, there were a few people who looked like me; Michael Jackson, when he was still Black (and not a pedophile), Bill Cosby (when he was not a rapist). Can I just admit here to being mad as hell that they couldn't keep it together and act right? Thank goodness for people like Denzel Washington, Chadwick Boseman, Oprah Winfrey, and Viola Davis.

If you think about the timing, though, it means for half my life, I didn't see myself represented at all. Things have gotten a bit better. Some programs seem to have a diversity checklist they complete before filming. I can't decide if that's an improvement, but I guess that's better than nothing. Even so, seeing people who represent my existence and experience of Blackness is relatively rare.

How Racism Compounds the Lack of Visibility

As usual, this is a non-exhaustive list; practically every Black person can recall a childhood experience of being othered. But it gives you an idea of how Black people experience the world. For many, the idea that they are other is reinforced by racism at school and in the streets.

By the time Black people get into the workplace, many have had a couple of decades' experience of racism and lack of representation. Racism in the workplace compounds what their lived experience tells them: that Black lives and Black perspectives don't matter. This is a mental health issue for Black people, and it's one we need to solve urgently.

But it's not just a problem for Black people; it's a problem for everyone. Because better representation means everyone gets a chance to see Black people as part of the norm, and that's a great way to fight racism.

Small Steps to Better Representation

So how do we fix this? Here are a few small starting points.

First, we need to normalize seeing Black people in all parts of life. My Medium friend Julia Hubbel does one small thing when she publishes content: she illustrates it with images of BIPOC. Sometimes such pictures are hard to find, but she does it anyway so that the people who read her content see Black people in everyday life. I think this is fabulous!

Second, think about your children's and grandchildren's bookshelves. Do you stick to the classics, or do you include books from across the spectrum, covering different ethnicities, gender expressions, and family situations?

I'm not pointing any fingers here. My daughter had more books with BIPOC characters than I did, but that's not saying a lot.

Third, actively seek out media that offer both diverse and positive representation. For young children, Sesame Street is a good start, but there are plenty of resources at the end of a Google search.

One practical thing I'm doing right now is helping to educate children about the impact of stereotypes, poor representation, and one-sided stories via the Anti-racism for Kids course I've created for Omnis Education.

As time goes on, I plan to expand on that and do my part to help create more equitable representation.

28
THE TALK: FIVE THINGS I TOLD MY DAUGHTER

Lessons in self-protection for my biracial child

"In the Caribbean, I'm mixed, but in the US, I'm Black," said my biracial daughter matter-of-factly.

She's not wrong.

While in the Caribbean her complexion may carry light-skin privilege (something she says she's still waiting to see evidence of), it also comes with accusations of not being Black enough, acting white, and talking white (as if white people have a monopoly on the excellent use of the English language).

As the descendant of language majors and writers, and as an early reader, my daughter can bend the English language to her will and is known for coming up with the right phrase at the right time.

But it's different when she leaves the Caribbean. In the US, she is Black, and since I'm the Black mother of a Black daughter, we've had to have the talk.

1. Don't Take an Item Away From Its Place

My daughter might have been a little older than most when we had the first part of the talk. She was seven or eight and tall for her age. We were shopping in Target, and she found an item she liked in the toy department and came rushing over to ladies' clothing to show it to me.

Hyper-alert, I looked around, and predictably, there was a security guard trying to make sure my excited child wasn't a potential thief. I took the item, walked back with her to the toy department and replaced it on its shelf. I explained that it was better for her to call me to look at an item than walk away with it.

2. Don't Look Like You Could Be Shoplifting

A few years later, in the UK, we had another part of the talk about avoiding the appearance of evil, if I can put it that way.

Specifically, I taught her that when she was browsing the shelves of any store, it was important not to look like she was about to put an item in her bag. She should walk in the middle of the shelves, and if she wanted to look at an item, she could. But she also had to be seen putting it back or putting it in the cart where it was visible.

3. Don't Approach the Exit Till You've Paid

Another lesson from that trip: don't walk toward the door unless you have paid for your items. As a Black person, I can't be sure you'll be granted the luxury of "forgetting to pay" that you'd probably get as a white person.

And if the alarm goes off as you head for the door, stop, find your receipt (I tend to keep it handy), and go back inside. Once you leave, you risk severe consequences. I don't want my daughter to end up arrested or dead because someone thought she was a thief or a threat. That was part three of the talk.

When I go shopping, I sometimes carry a backpack to store my purchases, but I never reach into it while I'm browsing the aisles. I use a trolley or shopping bag where everything is visible, and I'll only get out my wallet when I'm at the checkout. Again, I wouldn't want anyone deciding I'm trying to steal.

4. Don't Make Any Sudden Moves If Stopped by the Police

When my daughter decided to study in the US, we had a discussion of other rules. We'd watched *The Hate U Give* recently, as well as *When They See Us*, so the talk was top of mind. We talked about what to do if stopped by the police: keep your hands visible and ask for permission before reaching for anything.

In some ways, my daughter is lucky. Though she's a little taller than I am, she's definitely more girly. Where my once linear build; broad shoulders; and short, natural hair marked me as a potential male threat to old ladies at bus stops in the UK (especially when wearing a winter coat), it's unlikely that people will see my daughter the same way.

5. Be Better, Always

Still, as we know, women aren't safe even if they're sleeping in bed, so it's better to have the talk.

So I worry. Because she may not get the same response from law enforcement for even minding her own business or doing what white teens of a similar age do.

The most important part of the talk (aside from the parts that hopefully keep her alive) is that when you're Black, you have to be above reproach. It's a heavy burden to bear, but to be otherwise is far too dangerous — and could end in your death.

29
INTERNALIZED RACISM: THE ELEPHANT IN THE ROOM

An example of anti-Blackness in the Black community

One day, I shared a post on LinkedIn about a popular UK gym that had posted an inappropriate challenge for Black History Month, celebrated in October in the UK.

It was a workout challenge titled "12 Years of Slave," and the Instagram caption included the phrase "slavery was hard and so is this."

There is so much wrong with this that it's hard to know where to start:

- Using a film based on a true story of the horrors of enslavement as a marketing tool
- Likening a gym challenge to the enforced servitude of a people
- Letting that hot mess past the marketing gatekeepers so it ended up in public

But then the story got worse. It turned out that the person who had actually posted it was the Black man who managed that branch of the gym. As Black Americans say, "All skin folk ain't kinfolk."

One white colleague asked, "Is this still racism?" My answer: yes, it is. It's internalized anti-Black racism and bias. Sadly, that's also endemic in the Black community, but as with the rest of racism, the original sin belongs to white people. Let me explain.

*

Imagine you forcibly remove Black people from their African home countries, traffic them across the Atlantic, and enslave them. (Well, you don't have to imagine it; we all know it happened.)

You tell them everything about them is wrong and everything white is right. Social mobility and personal acceptability depend on proximity to whiteness. Getting a few personal benefits as a Black person depends on you upholding the same system that is oppressing your fellow Black people. You want to progress, so you go along with it.

Over generations, this becomes ingrained. Some people fight; others go along to get along.

Official enslavement ends, but nothing about the system really does. For generations, you have been denied a true account of your history and taught to hate your Black skin. Worse yet, you don't even realize it. Every time there's a qualifier in your description of a Black person and you repeat the value-laden phrases often heard in white mouths ("pretty for a Black girl," "articulate for a Black man," etc.), you reveal the depths of your self-hatred.

It's not totally your fault. It's how you were raised, and it takes a heck of a lot of unlearning.

*

As I've said before, this happens in every society the Europeans supposedly civilized. Whiteness remains the norm.

So that Black guy at the gym might not even have realized he was offending his fellow Black people and parading Black trauma for the gratification of the mostly white gym patrons.

Thank goodness somebody did and got the post taken down. But it should never have gotten that far.

I don't know how many other cases like this there are. It seems every few weeks, another brand puts out a marketing message or a product they really should have thought about more.

How do we stop incidents like this from happening? Here are a few things that occurred to me:

1) Teach all history to all people. A Black person who knows his history couldn't have pitched such a misguided and offensive campaign. And a gatekeeper who knows all of history couldn't go along with it.

2) We as Black people need to learn to love ourselves. Sometimes it's hard, because the world largely still says white is right, but let's work on that, OK?

3) Stop packaging Black trauma for entertainment.

4) Diversify your management, and make sure you don't just include the acceptable face of Blackness. No more tokenism. Include Black people who challenge you to do better and don't just go along with any half-baked idea so as not to rock the boat.

This isn't an exhaustive list, just a starting point, but we have to start somewhere. And we all have to do better.

30
LET'S TALK ABOUT BLACK JOY

Because it exists despite the doom and gloom

A friend said to me: "I know people need to know about experiences of racism, but they also need to know about the positivity in the community." And she was right.

For all that Black people suffer with racism and microaggressions, after suffering from enslavement and segregation, there are many moments of joy in a Black person's life. Here are a few of those:

Sometimes it's **when you catch the eye of someone who looks like you**. There's a world of empathy and understanding in a simple nod. For that brief moment, you see and are seen, and it's a balm to the spirit.

Sometimes it's **the triumph of achievement** at school or at work, of being the person in your family to excel, knowing that means you can lift others up, just as others have paved the way for you to rise.

Sometimes it's seeing how, through the generations, **your family has gained hard-won victories to improve your lot**. As the descendant of enslaved people, you've more than earned the right to bask in any success you gain.

Sometimes it's the **unfettered exhilaration of hanging with family and friends**, enjoying music, food, and company where you can be fully yourself in a way you can't when you're out in the white-majority world.

Sometimes it's knowing that the way you move in the world **inspires others like you**.

Sometimes it's seeing others who don't look like you **join in the anti-racism fight** — and the knowledge that you're not going it alone.

Sometimes it's **the fleeting moments when all's right with the world** and you feel like your full self, when you put the ills behind you and focus on the happiness.

Sure, sometimes being Black can be hard, especially for those existing in minoritized spaces. But sometimes it's joyous, and those kernels of joy let us survive the difficult times.

These are just a few examples, but there are others. We need to value those moments.

A wise woman said that in a world that tries to make Black people less than they are, **experiencing and showing joy is also an act of resistance and rebellion**. So let us feel that joy, then return to the fight.

GLOBAL BLACK ISSUES

This next sub-collection deals with issues affecting Black people in different parts of the world, from the passing of a beloved film star to what the 2020 US election tells us about racism.

31
MOURNING CHADWICK BOSEMAN AND THE BLACK PANTHER

Reflecting on the untimely passing of a Black hero

Already reeling from the multiple blows of racial injustice in the summer of 2020, the Black community worldwide mourned the untimely loss of Chadwick Boseman, an actor who personified persistence, grace, talent, and social conscience.

Aside from the loss of the man himself, which is crushing, we also were devastated by the loss of what Chadwick represented: the only chance many Black people have ever had to see a Black man on screen as a powerful hero and warrior king, untainted by racism, colonialism, and white saviorism.

His excellent work will continue to inspire us and our children, standing as a beacon in a world where, largely, Black people aren't viewed as being in charge of their own narrative.

I want to share this piece that I wrote just before seeing *Black Panther* for the first time.

*

The Promise of Black Panther

#Wakanda. As I wait to see the *Black Panther* movie (even on the small Caribbean island where I live, you have to buy tickets three days in advance to be sure of getting a seat), I am already blown away by its promise.

I'm neither a Marvel fan nor a superhero fan. In fact, I tend to shy away from comics brought to the big screen. This is a happy exception. I don't even care if the movie is good, though I'm reliably informed by those who've already scored tickets that it's not just good, it's great.

So why the excitement about this movie? In trying to explain it to some friends recently, I thought back to the many movies and TV shows I've seen in my 50-plus years of existence.

In the vast majority of them, there are very few people who look like me.

Where there *are* people who look like me, there's an overwhelming number of actors playing to stereotypes: slaves, servants, menial workers, prostitutes, drug dealers, criminals, miscellaneous thugs, and people destined to die in the first 10 minutes of the movie.

There are exceptions, played by some fine actors. But even in the 21st century, roles like the ones listed above seem more common than juicy, well-rounded parts.

For me — and for many others, I suspect — the world of *Black Panther* offers a tantalizing glimpse of a what-if world. What would Black people be like if they hadn't been enslaved, transplanted, and brutalized systemically across centuries?

A movie full of strong, proud, powerful people who look like me? If you're white, you probably take that sort of representation for granted. After all, it's the norm.

As a Black woman, I never will.

And be honest, if there were a gaping wound in your cultural psyche, wouldn't you want to see something that healed it, even a little bit?

I know I do.

*

As a Black woman, seeing that film was a balm to my soul, which is why I have seen it four times and will likely see it again. I know I'm not alone in that.

Rest in power, Chadwick Boseman. Thank you for the leadership and the inspiration. #Wakandaforever

#Blackexcellencematters

32
CELEBRATING THE BIDEN-HARRIS WIN, BUT MILLIONS OF AMERICANS VOTED FOR RACISM

We got the right result, but we anti-racists still have a *lot* of work to do!

Like many of you, I celebrated the victory of Joe Biden and Kamala Harris in the 2020 US election.

I also celebrated the fact that a Black and Indian American woman will be in the White House. To be honest, I thought Barack Obama was the only melanated person I'd see there in my lifetime. So, yes, I was ecstatic, because representation matters. Many little girls will see Harris there and know that they, too, have a shot.

But I'm also mindful that we have work to do. A *lot* of work.

Many people hoped that the 2020 US election would be a categorical vote against racism, climate change denial, children in cages, dismantled environmental protections, and a mishandled pandemic.

It wasn't.

Not even close.

Instead, the race went down to the wire, with no early indication of which vision of the future would win: white supremacy and patriarchy, or equity and humane treatment for all. In the end, Biden and Harris prevailed (thank goodness), but it shouldn't even have been a question.

What's pretty clear is that tens of millions of people — nearly half of all Americans — voted *for* racism.

Are you surprised? I'm not. White supremacy stops at nothing, and one of its promoters in chief has had a huge platform for four years.

I've never trusted him. The orange one showed me who he was in a televised interview in the '80s, and I've been wary of him since then. Everything I've seen since confirms I was right to be. His own xenophobia aside, he's emboldened other racists to come out in the open. It's been a difficult four years, even for those, like me, watching from the sidelines.

Most Black people weren't fooled, either. Black writers and activists like Marley K. warned that racism would be on the ballot for this election — and that it just might win. So they did their bit to fight the racist tide.

According to a *New York Times* voter demographic report, Black people put their vote where their mouth was, and 90 percent of Black women supported the Biden-Harris ticket. Black men avoided the Kanye effect, and more than 80 percent of them also voted for Biden and Harris. (I'm showing serious side-eye to the Black people who voted the other way, though.)

Indigenous people also turned out in huge numbers to vote for Biden and Harris (respect to the Navajo Nation, who had a huge [and decisive] turnout for Biden and Harris).

No ethnic group is a monolith, and this was clear with the Latinx vote. As Lisa Hurley points out in our second *Introvert Sisters* US election special, that identity encompasses people who are American born and raised through multiple generations as well as those with more recent origins in a slew of countries throughout South and Central America and the Caribbean. Still, the majority of Latinx people voted for Biden and Harris. (More side-eye to those who didn't.)

So now let's look at the white folks. Well, they're not a monolith, either, and while plenty voted the right way, that contingent couldn't totally undermine the tens of millions representing the "white is right" brigade.

Unsurprisingly, old white men voted for the status quo, for the rich getting richer, and for not giving up any of the privileges they'd carved out of the sweat and labor of Black people and the genocide of Indigenous peoples.

One of my friends was disappointed that people who identify as Christian would vote for someone who had done so many unchristian things. Bye-bye, Ten Commandments; hello, lying, cheating, coveting, and worse.

It was also disappointing that more white women voted for the orange one this time round than they did before. And this time, they knew exactly who and what they were voting for, which blows my mind. Talk about cutting off your nose to spite your face (an evocative British expression that seems particularly apt when you consider the patriarchal values most of the orange one's followers espouse).

I'm no statistician, but if you compare the numbers of white people expressing "support" for Black Lives Matter and diversity, equity, and inclusion initiatives to the numbers of white voters voting against those very things, it all adds up to a bunch of performative allyship. Millions of people are lying.

Clearly, if you're reading this, you're not one of those voters, but perhaps, like me, you realize that we're only getting started with fighting racism. The racists walk among us, and they are getting bolder. The Biden-Harris victory won't make us unsee the ugliness of the last four years, and the outright racism that killed so many people in 2020 alone.

The bottom line is that the 2020 US election is *not* a triumph of sanity and humanity. Since tens of millions of Americans don't see racism, xenophobia, and bigotry as deal breakers, the election reinforces whose lives don't matter to them.

Far from living in a post-racial society, as many would like — no, *love* — to believe, Americans are living in a racist society. And Black people are existing in a racist world (UK and Europe, you don't get off scot-free, either). As I said, we have a lot of work to do.

America may not be taken quite as seriously anymore, but it still has a major place in the world. What happens there matters to other people. Undo climate protections, and small nations suffer. Close your borders and reduce innovation and creativity. Support the racists over the race abused (I stole that from Catherine Pugh), and you state unequivocally that Black lives will never matter to you.

It's disheartening.

But what does give me hope is that the passage of time will eliminate many of those who voted against humanity. And the passage of time will soon give the youth who care about the planet a bigger say. The work we are doing every day is helping to create a better future. And the 2020 election result gives us the chance for a little more sanity and breathing room while we continue to fight necessary battles and make good trouble in service of that future.

Meanwhile, my dear active anti-racists (because you know I love to give us all homework, lol), find your people who are willing to listen and slap them upside their head with some truth about our racist world. Show them by example that more for all doesn't shrink the pot; it enriches it.

And recognize that the 2020 US election reveals that it's more important than ever to do the hard, painful work of dismantling racist structures, of undermining racist ideals, of resisting efforts to reduce diversity. To do otherwise would be unthinkable.

33
HOW CELEBRATING CHRISTMAS WHILE BLACK CAUSED A RUCKUS

Examining the racism behind the trolling of Sainsbury's 2020 Christmas ad

In 2020, if you wanted proof that anti-Black racism is everywhere, you had only to look at the vitriol spewed by commenters after the release of the Sainsbury's Christmas video ad in the UK.

The content of the ad is pretty unobjectionable. It features a daughter talking to her dad about enjoying gravy and roasted potatoes on Christmas Day. And there are stills of Christmases past throughout the one-minute video.

Sounds good, right? You'd think it was guaranteed to give viewers the warm and fuzzies and stir up some pleasant holiday feelings.

Well, not so fast. While some people of all hues loved the ad, a lot of white Brits didn't. The reason? Because the family featured in the ad was Black.

Many of the white people who commented negatively felt that:

- There were no British people in the ad (clearly, Black Brits don't count for them)
- Since it was a Black family, the dad portrayed probably wasn't the father of the children (I kid you not, someone actually said this)

- It was disgusting and grounds for a boycott of the supermarket chain (I can't even)

The bottom line: celebrating Christmas while Black is somehow out of the ordinary.

As a Black woman, I loved the ad. I was happy that, for once, Black Brits could see themselves represented in an everyday experience, where the color of their skin was incidental. Many of the Black commenters agreed.

Though many UK programs now have diverse casts (another huge bone of contention for some commenters), often, the fact of Blackness or brownness is part of the storyline with these characters. It was great to see that the Sainsbury's ad avoided this, as Alicia Adejobi said in *Metro*: "It was beautiful to see people with my skintone on TV but it was just as beautiful that, for once, it wasn't 'about' them being Black."

Racism and Representation

But, clearly, surprising not a single Black or brown person, the UK still has a deep and often unacknowledged problem with anti-Black racism and bias.

Many non-melanated Brits are happy to talk about how Britain ended the trade in enslaved Africans, but less happy to talk about the racial power dynamics resulting from colonialism that still affect Black people's experiences in the country and around the world today.

The reaction to the ad illustrates the now common saying that for those accustomed to privilege, equality looks like oppression.

While there have been more diverse casts on screen in recent years, if you think about the history of television in the UK, most programs have featured white people. It seems hard that Black people shouldn't be allowed a single one-minute ad without stirring up venom.

Plus, this ad was just one of a series of three from the supermarket chain. Another ad featured a white family. I have yet to hear of any Black or brown people objecting to that. For us, lack of representation is the norm, and some of us may not even notice it explicitly. However, we *do* notice and appreciate when we are represented.

I found it interesting that one person chose to question the family dynamics. Clearly, far too many dysfunctional Black families are shown in the media, and not enough functional ones. As I've said before, and I'll say again, representation matters.

Myths and Stereotypes

Funmi Olutoye wrote about the controversy in the *Independent* and made a few good points, including

- People are uncomfortable confronting the myth that the UK isn't racist (yes, of course, it is)
- People were afraid that this ad was the tip of the iceberg that would lead to a Black supremacy that operates the same way white supremacy has (Don't worry; we just want equity, but if

that's what people think, maybe it's time to rethink white supremacy?)

- People seem to want to see Black people only in certain stereotypical roles and settings (I guess the ad was far too normal.)

Olutoye says, "If that means [Black people are] in the places where you typically only see white people and you have an issue with that, then you are part of the problem. Inclusion is not supremacy.[i]"

So where do we go from here? I applaud Sainsbury's for making the effort to diversify its Christmas advertising (though I notice its management team is not diverse) and for avoiding the obvious stereotypes of Black people. And I'm happy for all those Black Brits who saw people like them on their screens for Christmas.

But the racist backlash revealed that there's still a lot of work to do before an ad like this is seen as just as normal as an ad with an all-white cast. It would be great if the next time this happens, we can all get warm holiday feelings without feeling the chill of racism.

AFTERWORD: I'M STILL WAITING (FOR RACISM TO END)

In the wake of yet another incident where an unarmed Black man was shot by the police, I wrote the following. Believe it or not, it was going to be an essay, then it took a turn. That happens. It seems a fitting way to end this collection.

It's been 3 months since George Floyd

and here we are again.

In that time, many others have died

unremarked by the headlines

and therefore by us

That's why I'm still waiting

for Black lives to matter

I'm still waiting

for Black people to be able to walk tall at work,

knowing that they will be valued appropriately, or at least equally

knowing that nobody will touch their hair, question their education, or doubt their experience

I'm still waiting

to walk into every shop and be a valued customer

not to feel the question mark above my head

while sensing the suspicious breath of the security guard

I'm still waiting

for the day when I don't have to have the talk

about how to survive an encounter with the US police

and emerge both alive and free

I'm still waiting for being Black *not* to be a crime

so we can own nice things and live in nice places

without being questioned or arrested

I'm still waiting to see real action affirm Black people's rightful place

in countries built on our blood, sweat, and tears

and I mean that literally

I'm still waiting for healthcare, housing, and education

to offer Black people equal care and attention, equal opportunity

and an equal chance of not just surviving, but thriving

I'm still waiting for reparation and redress

Didn't my ancestors earn it

several times over?

I'm still waiting to throw off the shackles

for society to remove the straitjacket

that keeps us bonded though no longer enslaved

I'm still waiting for Martin Luther King's dream

to wake, within us all

but I think I'll be waiting a long, long time

so, I'm still waiting for Black lives to really matter

I'm still waiting to be free

BIBLIOGRAPHY

1. While Black: Thoughts on the Assumption of Wrongness

Said, E. (n.d.). *Edward W. Said Quotes.* Goodreads. Available at: https://www.goodreads.com/author/quotes/16770310.Edward_W_Said [accessed Nov. 28, 2020].

Woods, S. *The Other Columbus: Anti-Racism Work Is Supposed to Be Hard.* Columbus Alive. Available at www.columbusalive.com/story/entertainment/human-interest/2020/06/03/other-columbus-anti-racism-work-is-supposed-to-be-hard/43290249/ [accessed Dec. 17, 2021].

DuVernay, A. Dir. (2016). *13TH.* Netflix. Available at: https://www.imdb.com/title/tt5895028/ [accessed Nov. 28, 2020].

3. Let's Discard the Notion

Pugh, C. (2020). *There Is No Such Thing as a "White Ally" — "TNSWA" Part I.* Medium. Available at: https://medium.com/we-defeat-the-enemies-we-define/there-is-no-such-thing-as-a-white-ally-469bb82799f2 [accessed Nov. 28, 2020].

6. Do Black Lives Really Matter?

Associated Press. (2020). *Grand Jury Indicts 1 Police Officer in Breonna Taylor Death..* Available at: https://www.kktv.com/2020/09/23/grand-jury-indicts-1-police-officer-in-breonna-taylor-death-no-homicide-charges/.

Mapping Police Violence. (2014). *National Trends.* Available at: https://mappingpoliceviolence.org/nationaltrends.

8. Black Lives Matter and the Barbadian Context

Hurley Hall, S. (2020). *Exploring Shadeism — One Year On.* Available at: https://antiracism.substack.com/p/exploring-shadeism-one-year-on [accessed Nov. 28, 2020].

Monuments and Memorials to Horatio Nelson, 1st Viscount Nelson (note 11). Wikipedia. Available at https://en.wikipedia.org/wiki/Monuments_and_memorials_to_Horatio_Nelson,_1st_Viscount_Nelson#cite_note-11 [accessed Dec. 17, 2021].

10. Six Reasons to Raise Your BIPOC Kids in Black-Majority Countries

Booth, R. (2019). *"Institutional Racism": 20 Years Since Stephen Lawrence Inquiry. The Guardian.* Available at: https://www.theguardian.com/uk-news/2019/feb/22/institutional-racism-britain-stephen-lawrence-inquiry-20-years.

Sian, K. (n.d.). *Extent of Institutional Racism in British Universities Revealed Through Hidden Stories.* The Conversation. Available at: https://theconversation.com/extent-of-institutional-racism-in-british-universities-revealed-through-hidden-stories-118097.

Holroyd, J. (2019). *Implicit Racial Bias and the Anatomy of Institutional Racism.* Centre for Crime and Justice Studies. Available at: https://www.crimeandjustice.org.uk/publications/cjm/article/implicit-racial-bias-and-anatomy-institutional-racism.

Gragg, Sanya Whittaker. (2020). *To My Beautiful Black Sons: Come Home ALIVE.* Medium. Available at: https://medium.com/illumination/to-my-beautiful-black-sons-come-home-alive-fad1b34c8795 [accessed Nov. 28, 2020].

18. Oh, the Gaslighting

Stevens Alder, R. (2020). *I Don't See That I Am Black, You Do.* Medium. Available at: https://medium.com/illumination-curated/i-dont-see-that-i-am-black-you-do-c1e67e306a18 [accessed Nov. 28, 2020].

Mergen, O. (2020). *Seemingly Harmless Racist Phrases to Avoid Around Your BIPOC*

Friends. Medium. Available at: https://medium.com/an-injustice/seemingly-harmless-racist-phrases-to-avoid-around-your-bipoc-friends-e4f770e31319 [accessed Nov. 28, 2020].

19. Race and the Freelance Writer, Revisited

Fanon, F. (2016). *The Fact of Blackness*. N.p.: Moor's Head Press, 2016.

20. Hair So Problematic

CROWN Coalition. (2014). Homepage. The CROWN Act, SB 188. Available at: https://www.thecrownact.com/.

21. Seen yet Unseen

Hurley Hall, S. (2020). *Meet Marley K., Anti-Racism Writer*. Available at: https://www.antiracismnewsletter.com/p/meet-marley-k-anti-racism-writer [accessed Nov. 28, 2020].

22. Building a Business While Black — It's Not So Easy

Rogers, T.N. (2020). *There Are 607 Billionaires in the United States, and Only 5 of Them Are Black. Business Insider*. Available at: https://www.businessinsider.com/black-billionaires-in-the-united-states-2020-2.

Horsey, D. (2014). *The American Dream Game*. Twitter. Available at https://twitter.com/consentbaby/status/520361693776326656.

American Civil Liberties Union. (2019). *School-to-Prison Pipeline*. Available at: https://www.aclu.org/issues/juvenile-justice/school-prison-pipeline.

Elias, M. (2013). *The School-to-Prison Pipeline*. Teaching Tolerance. Available at: https://www.tolerance.org/magazine/spring-2013/the-school-to-prison-pipeline.

Scott-Clayton, J., and Li, J. (2016). *Black-White Disparity in Student Loan Debt More Than Triples After Graduation.* Brookings. Available at: https://www.brookings.edu/research/black-white-disparity-in-student-loan-debt-more-than-triples-after-graduation/.

Lemmons, K. Dir. (2020). *Self Made: Inspired by the Life of Madam C.J. Walker.* Available at: https://www.imdb.com/title/tt8771910/ [accessed Sep. 25, 2019].

24. Black Women, Stereotypes, and Fetishes

Lartey, S. (2019). *The Jezebel Sticker.* Medium. Available at aninjusticemag.com/the-jezebel-sticker-2fcb1149765c [accessed Dec. 17, 2021].

Smith, J. (2019). *For Toni Morrison, Who Taught Me to See. Rolling Stone.* Available at: https://www.rollingstone.com/culture/culture-features/toni-morrison-author-beloved-tribute-868572/.

Pilgrim, D. (2012). *The Jezebel Stereotype.* Jim Crow Museum of Racist Memorabilia, Ferris State University. Available at: https://www.ferris.edu/jimcrow/jezebel/.

Atanmo, G. Instagram. Available at https://www.instagram.com/glographics/?hl=en.

Kobo. (2020). *14 Books for Getting Smarter About Anti-racism.* Medium. Available at: https://medium.com/@KoboBooks/14-books-for-getting-smarter-about-anti-racism-25aaf3503b6d [accessed Nov. 28, 2020].

27. The Battle for Representation Starts in Childhood

Hubbel, J. *Julia Hubbel.* Walkabout Saga. Available at www.walkaboutsaga.com/author/julia-hubbel/ [accessed Dec. 17, 2021].

28. The Talk: Five Things I Told My Daughter

Tillman, G. Dir. (2018). *The Hate U Give.* IMDb. Available at:

https://www.imdb.com/title/tt5580266/.

DuVernay, A. Dir. (2019). *When They See Us.* Available at: https://www.imdb.com/title/tt7137906/.

32. Celebrating the Biden-Harris Win, but Millions of Americans Voted *for* Racism

National Exit Polls: How Different Groups Voted. (n.d.). *The New York Times.* Available at: https://www.nytimes.com/interactive/2020/11/03/us/elections/exit-polls-president.html.

The Introvert Sisters. (2020). *2020 Election: The Battle for the White House, Ep. 4.* Available at: https://theintrovertsisters.com/2020-election-battle/ [accessed Nov. 28, 2020].

Hurley Hall, S. (2020). *Meet Marley K., Anti-Racism Writer.* Available at: https://www.antiracismnewsletter.com/p/meet-marley-k-anti-racism-writer [accessed Nov. 28, 2020].

Hurley Hall, S. (2020). *Meet Catherine Pugh, Esq., Anti-Racism Writer.* Available at: https://www.antiracismnewsletter.com/p/meet-catherine-pugh-esq-anti-racism [accessed Nov. 28, 2020].

33. How Celebrating Christmas While Black Caused a Ruckus

Sainsbury's. (2020). Twitter. Available at: https://twitter.com/sainsburys/status/1327506558322880514 [accessed Nov. 28, 2020].

Adejobi, A. (2020). *Black People in a Sainsbury's Christmas Advert Shouldn't Make Your Blood Boil. Metro.* Available at: https://metro.co.uk/2020/11/17/black-people-in-a-sainsburys-christmas-advert-shouldnt-make-you-angry-13608767/ [accessed Nov. 28, 2020].

Olutoye, F. (2020). *Opinion: The Fury Over the Sainsbury's Ad With a Black Family*

Proves the UK Is Still Shockingly Racist. The Independent. Available at: https://www.independent.co.uk/voices/sainsburys-christmas-advert-black-family-racism-b1724922.html.

ABOUT THE AUTHOR

Sharon Hurley Hall (she, her) is an anti-racism activist, writer, and educator. Firmly committed to doing her part to eliminate racism, she is the founder and curator-in-chief of *Sharon's Anti-Racism Newsletter* (https://www.antiracismnewsletter.com). In this weekly online publication, Sharon writes about existing while Black in majority-white spaces and amplifies the voices of other anti-racism activists. She has written and ghostwritten articles for companies and nonprofits looking to show up authentically with their diversity, equity, inclusion, belonging and racial and social justice content. Sharon is also the Head of Anti-Racism for Diverse Leaders Group.

A writer with more than 25 years' experience, Sharon is the author of *Exploring Shadeism*, an analysis of colorism in Barbados and the wider Caribbean. A self-confessed word nerd and polymath, Sharon has also worked as a journalist, an editor, and a senior journalism professor at Coventry University in the UK , where she also helped develop the MA journalism program. A speaker and podcaster, Sharon is the co-host of *The Introvert Sisters* podcast and has been a featured presenter at events by the National Collaboration for Youth Mental Health, SIETAR DC, The Equality Practice, and Jim-Ree Museum Inc.

Sharon holds MA degrees in media and cultural studies, and in teaching and learning in higher education.

Made in the USA
Monee, IL
14 May 2023

33576248R00095